UNSHACKLED QUEEN

From Heartbreak to Wholeness

C. RUTH TAYLOR

Extra MILE Innovators
Kingston, Jamaica W.I.

Published by
Extra MILE Innovators
54 Montgomery Avenue, Kingston 10, Jamaica W.I.
www.extramileja.com
ruthtaylor@extramileja.com
extramileinnovators@gmail.com

Cover Design and Illustrations by Rachel Wade-Moss

AUTHOR CONTACT
For speaking engagements, conferences, workshops, Indie publishing, mentoring and career coaching services, contact the author at
ruthtaylor@extramileja.com.

FREE PUBLISHING STARTERKIT
Download these two publishing resources from our website
www.authorprenuersecrets.com.

PRAISE FOR 'UNSHACKLED QUEEN"

God does not waste experiences and neither should we. Ruth Taylor epitomizes what is meant by 'experience teaches wisdom' and 'a caterpillar becoming a butterfly.' Her life demonstrates that one does not have to be a product of their society but that faith in God has the power to truly TRANSFORM lives. As you read through the pages of *Unshackled Queen*, I hope that it will help you in finding true liberation, self-acceptance and wholeness that only comes through faith in Jesus Christ as your Lord and Saviour! Enjoy!

Shauna-Gay Gregory-Edwards
Forensic Psychologist

Unshackled Queen speaks volumes about transparency, trials, truth, and triumph... The revelation of the length and breadth of the experiences that Ruth has had, testify to the fact that trials are in fact, part and parcel of the believer's journey. Her faithful Heavenly Father has used her experiences to fashion her into a pearl which clearly reflects the glory of the Son of God... Like Yvette, she seems positioned to face her future trials with the song of triumph that believers in Christ are "... hard pressed on every side, but not crushed; perplexed, but not in despair; persecuted, but not abandoned; struck down, but not destroyed" (2 Corinthians 4:8,9).

Dr. Zoe Simpson, Executive Director
Women Centre of Jamaica Foundation

———◦O•———

There is no question about the fact that the environment and family experiences of our early years most times will determine whether we fail or succeed in our ability to cope with life challenges, make sound decisions and achieve real success in our adult years. Ruth, all in one stroke, tells us a true story like a novel and uses her gift of teaching to provide us with Biblical solutions to overcoming the impact of adverse early childhood and adolescent experiences. Born out of Ruth's own testimony of having overcome, Unshackled Queen is a great work and a must-read for everyone... it will impact you and the way you relate to others.

John Roomes
CEO, Wycliffe Caribbean Bible Translators

———◦O•———

Painful episodes from our past often unconsciously imprison us in self-destructive attitudes and behaviours, born out of fear and the need to be loved and accepted. Ruth's writing is vivid, her ideas clear, and the story shared provides hope for all of us who wrestle with life issues from our painful past. Ruth's own walk through the difficult land of forgiveness and her experience of the healing that comes with that journey is a clear vindication that the biblical way of the Lord provides for us the best way for resolving the most intractable of interpersonal relationships. This is a well-written work."

David Pearson, Former Academic Dean
Jamaica Theological Seminary

Ruth Taylor has been, and remains an enigma in my life as one who pursues God with diligence and worshipful fervour. She has given of herself selflessly to the cause of bringing Christ to the lost with effortless ease, dedication and commitment. Her encounters with 'love' have yielded much heartaches and brokenness, but I now concur, not without purpose.

She now pens a book reflective of her personal pain and healing to once more help others to heal, and to show that the greater the magnitude of your pain, as you continue to trust God despite the heartache, the greater blessing you can derive, and the greater blessing you can become. *Unshackled Queen* is not only for the broken hearted but for those of us who will be heartbroken and propelled to greater love as we read and resolve to find purpose in the pain

Rev. Dr. Carla Dunbar, J.P
Pastor, Author & Marriage Counsellor

NOTES

DISCLAIMER

This is a work of non-fiction. It reflects a true story although the names of people and places have been changed to maintain privacy or prevent embarrassment. Some events have been compressed and some dialogues recreated.

To: Rev. Courtney Richards (Pops), your prayer has been answered

FOREWORD

---◆○◆---

Everyone loves a story! Stories are part of the fabric of life. Indeed, some people argue that life is a story; a tale of who we are and how we grow and develop. Each person's story affects those around them. Your story affects my story and my story yours and on and on it goes. As a result, we are shaped by each other's story in ways that we might not even know. But it is good to know so that we can re-write the narratives of our lives as we need to.

Some stories are good and some are simply awful! I especially like the good ones. Good stories breathe a life of their own. They not only have an enthralling or gripping plot that keeps the attention of the reader or listener but they have impact - they leave you with much to think about and do to change or improve yourself in significant ways. In this regard, I particularly like stories of hope, hope built on perseverance and resilience! I like to read and hear of others who have overcome the odds through the dark and awful circumstances of life.

For we all have dark and awful circumstances no matter how sunny life has been for us! So, when I read of someone who has pressed on, who has a "never say die" or a "never give up" attitude, a winning attitude as author John Maxwell calls it, it gets my attention. It steels my resolve in dealing with and overcoming the struggles of my life like the necessary or unnecessary losses or the failures and rejections of others, or the abuses and excesses that I have had to face.

Such is the story Ruth shares, in this gripping and pulsating recollection and examination of Yvette's life and times. I know Ruth well! She, after all, is my spiritual daughter. She has been transparent and vulnerable in sharing episodes of her life with me and others, her confidantes.

She speaks with refreshing authenticity. Her personal story is revealing and riveting; transparent and transformative. Here's a woman, a young woman, who has had myriad failures and distresses in relationships - attempted rape, rejection, betrayal, broken promises, lack of love and one painful incident after another that it takes the breath away!

But instantly one is brought back to hold on and look deeper. For, here is a woman who has not caved in to the overwhelming disasters and tragedies of personal relationships. Here's a woman who has beaten the odds and has triumphed like a colossal warrior, which she is, and is not a mere survivor, but a teacher and exhorter on how to deal life's tragedies a deathly blow: to win in and through faith in God.

Some readers may not like that: her faith in God! But hang on! This is not a wishy-washy faith or a mealy-mouthed experience or expression of faith. This is enduring and transforming faith. This is robust, dynamic and muscular faith!

In this book, Ruth shows that faith is not incidental or tangential to one's triumph but that it is central to overcoming tragedies, wounds and pain. She painstakingly and with the precision of a surgeon, not only tells a story but analyses and examines it, calling forth and teasing out what makes for a survivor. I think the honest reader will want to know how and why she has triumphed. If this story is going to matter and matter to you, you must allow what worked for Yvette – the source and reservoir of her triumph and healing – to work for you. It has worked its transforming power on me. I hope it will do so for you!

Rev. Courtney Richards,
Mentor, Global Missionary and Psychologist

CONTENTS

———◆◆◆———

INTRODUCTION

"Yet God has made everything beautiful for its own time.
He has planted eternity in the human heart, but even so, people cannot see the whole scope of God's work from beginning
to end" (Ecclesiastes 3:11).

Painful journeys can lead to beautiful destinations. The story you're about to read is true although pseudonyms have been used to protect the identities of some of the persons involved. It is a fascinating tale of how God transformed the life a broken young woman by the name of Yvette into something beautiful.

Yvette's journey towards liberation, self-acceptance and wholeness is an example of hope for those who have experienced broken romantic and parental relationships.

The author creatively uses her story to teach the pathway to wholeness and how we can find purpose in pain. *Unshackled Queen* is a mentoring and teaching tool designed to bring liberation and consolation to those who have experienced terrible emotional losses and are struggling to cope and find hope.

Yvette's story brings to light the ill effects of fatherlessness, teenage pregnancy, suicide and depression. *Unshackled Queen* calls us to responsible parenting and to walk the difficult path of forgiveness.

Finally, in the closing section of the book, the author provides 21 secrets and practical steps to overcome adversity and experience wholeness. You will discover the markers of wholeness, and locate where you are on your journey to wholeness.

Unshackled Queen shows there is hope for the brokenhearted because God sees your tears, and if you trust Him, He will wipe them all away and turn your experience into something glorious.

PART I:

THE MAKING OF A HEARTBREAK QUEEN

1.

NOTORIOUS BEGINNINGS

"Everything in adulthood can be traced back to childhood." −Penny Junior

"TRUTH IS STRANGER THAN FICTION"

The gentleman remarked, "Yvette, you did bad enuh. You memba when you did drop inna di pit?" ("Yvette you were such a bad child. Do you remember when you fell into the pit?"). How could she forget? Yvette remembered and clearly was not amused.

She, therefore, kept a low profile for the rest of the evening at the family's Christmas gathering.

Unpacking the events of Yvette's early childhood has been a significant part of her journey to liberation and wholeness. The earliest memories of her childhood were not pleasant, and for many years she wondered if they were fictitious but her father and grandaunt and others confirmed that they were not. This reality was not an easy pill to swallow.

On Yvette's first visit with the family overseas, someone at their Christmas gathering took the liberty of reminding her of her early notoriety as a precocious five-year old. Prior to this gentleman's question, Yvette was often plagued by the memory of those very words whenever she visited the family during the holidays as a child. Just like at the Christmas gathering, whenever she introduced herself, the first words out of the mouths of people were: "Oh, Yvette, the likkle bad pickni, weh use to live with Aunt Merl." ("Oh you are Yvette; the bad, little child who used to live with Aunt Merl").

How did a child less than six years old develop notoriety? I believe there were plausible reasons for Yvette being labelled a "bad" child. In the Jamaican context, strong-willed and stubborn little children are often labelled as 'bad.' At that time, Yvette was an extroverted, strong willed, adventurous and even disobedient child. She often recalled some of her childhood adventurous exploits which no doubt contributed to her notoriety.

Yvette was the only child living in a household with adults: her father, grandaunt, cousin and uncle. She was desperately seeking friendship with people her age. This need was evident when she stopped to play with friends when sent on errands. Yvette also went next door to swing on the neighbour's swing despite being told otherwise. And yes, how could she forget exploring the landscape with her friend Tash and falling into that newly constructed pit?

It's a miracle that Yvette did not die or hurt herself. You can only imagine how scared the family was, so much so, that to this day, people recall the event three decades later.

On the other hand, children are naturally curious, fearless and quite active in early childhood. It is to be expected that they will flirt with danger. They have few fears at this stage. They are merely exploring their world, trying to understand it. The difference is that her tendency for exploration seemed to have become embroiled in a fatal situation, and hence the horrendous label, "Bad Yvette." After these events, her life was never the same. Her notoriety was irreversible, and her emotions became almost irrevocably damaged in early childhood.

2.

EMOTIONAL DAMAGE

"For as he thinketh in his heart, so is he..."
(Proverbs 23:7).

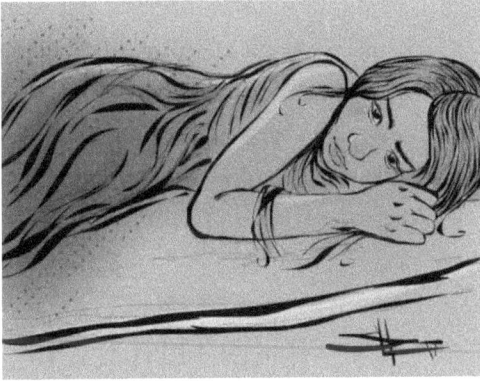

A s a result of Yvette's notoriety, some 'false belief viruses' entered and became lodged in her heart. They were deeply embedded and unconsciously destroying her life system. Some of these viruses seemed to have superhuman strength and like kryptonite to Superman, they were killing her. Yvette was unconsciously engaged in self-destructive behaviours and suffering a slow death. She was a wounded soul from early childhood and in the ensuing years; there were many life experiences that multiplied those wounds, providing a firm footing for the viruses. These viruses needed to be uprooted and brought to the surface of her memory system (her mind), in order to be dealt with.

However, her external accomplishments kept them hidden. Yvette's congenial demeanour and appropriate behaviour in public kept them secure in their hiding place. Behind closed doors away from the eye of all but her Creator, it was a different story. She constantly cried and was terribly fearful. She pleaded with God for help and strength to face each day or requested death. Yvette remembers there were times when she hid under the bed to cry, keeping her pain in obscurity. She did not want anyone to know how badly she was hurting.

TURBULENT TEENS

Yvette hated her life and developed a strong love affair with death once she hit the turbulent teen years; the time when our struggle for identity is at its peak. This is the time our bodies are changing, strange hormones are pulsating through them and we are trying to figure out our bodies and the meaning of life. Yvette suffered from panic attacks and was deathly afraid of public activities, unfamiliar surroundings and people. Timidity had gotten hold of her. It robbed Yvette of her voice, and sentenced her to her own private prison of solitary confinement. This prison had tormenting guards of negative self-destructive thoughts.

It did not help that Yvette's mother was so overprotective, and did not let her go anywhere after 6 p.m. including church. She would often say, "Be home by 6 p.m. A coulda iivn King Jesus, mi se yu fi come home by 6 o' clock." (Be home by 6 p.m. Even if you are out with even Jesus himself, you must be home by 6 p.m.). This stance meant no social events or church activities after 6 p.m. This pattern continued until Yvette was 17 years old.

Although this was protective, it made Yvette naive to the ways of the world. Her sense of isolation and lack of exposure made her reticent and laconic. Her moods were mercurial. There were days when she was like a zombie in her home and angry for no apparent reason. She refused to speak to anyone. She was suffering silently and did not even know why. Yvette experienced constant mood swings.

After careful consideration, Yvette identified and shared the main belief system viruses that were unconsciously creating havoc in her life. They were not unique to her.

I trust that as you read, if you can relate to any of these viruses, you will also recognize them for what they are and seek to eliminate them from your life before they destroy you. Yvette's viruses were:

- I am unwanted and unloved echoed by the thought: "nobody loves me."
- I am black, undesirable and ugly.
- I am inferior to others because of my colour and social class.
- I am a bad person. I can do nothing right, no matter how hard I try.
- Nobody stays; there must be something wrong with me.
- My life has no meaning.
- I am not valuable or worthy of being loved.
- Perhaps if I do right, and excel I will be loved.
- I need to be and do things perfectly to be accepted and affirmed.
- I won't be happy for long, "chicken merri, hawk deh near."
- If I am happy, unhappiness is lurking around the corner. Something will soon go wrong.
- My opinion does not matter.
- I need to prove that I am good enough to earn my blessings.
- I am an "intelligent idiot" having only capital sense.
- God is ashamed of me.
- I am deeply ashamed of myself.

Along with those belief viruses were underlying fears, anger, resentment and un-forgiveness. Most of these were directed at her mother. Her mom was a martinet and her disciplinary approach, and parenting style cemented those belief systems, resulting in more damage to her emotions. Yvette's mom was a firm believer in corporal punishment, as most Jamaicans were at that time. The corporal punishment was painful but even deadlier were her words; especially being called an "intelligent idiot." Everything had to be done perfectly. Her mantra was, "Only the best (perfection) was good enough."

The irony is that hurting people hurt others. Yvette's mother was unaware that she was meting out this type of behaviour because she herself had experienced significant wounding. She was battling her own demons from a life of abuse and rejection and following a pattern she had observed.

FAMILY PATTERNS

By the age of thirteen, Yvette's mom was on her own fending for herself and moving from home to home. At the age of seventeen she became pregnant with Yvette, the offspring of a teenager who did not have a clue about parenting. A few years after giving birth, Yvette's mom sent her to live with her father and his family where she stayed until Aunt Merl's death. Afterward, Yvette lived with her maternal grandmother in another parish and would visit her mom in Kingston over the summer holidays. Eventually, things improved for her mom and when Yvette was ten years old, she began living permanently with her mom. Over the years, Yvette's mom did the best she could but during those years, Yvette thought she was cruel and wanted to escape. Her happiest moments were those away from home.

Things were too unpredictable at home. She never knew when she would be yelled at or when a prolonged quarrel would ensue over what Yvette or her siblings had done wrong. Yvette lived in a constant state of uneasiness and anxiety. Many times she felt like running away but never had the courage to do so.

Thankfully this is not the end of their story. The relationship between mother and daughter has been healed. Today, we are amazed how much God has transformed their relationship. Yvette sees her mom almost weekly and they talk about everything. They can stay in the same room for days and Yvette does not feel like escaping from her. They do ministry together and are now a strong team.

3.

SUICIDAL IDEATION

"Never, never, never give up."
—Sir Winston Churchill

In those early years, Yvette was ignorant of the thought viruses affecting her and oblivious to the fact that subsequent wounding experiences had impaired her judgment. This resulted in over compensation in many areas, and the development of perfectionist tendencies. Yvette became a doer-driven, workaholic and chronic people pleaser. She was also in a constant conundrum with her dad's absence and rejection. "Why does he not want me; what did I do wrong?"

Fear became a controlling factor in her life; fear of people, fear of success, fear of failure, and fear of insects just to name a few. The only thing she did not fear was death. The story of how these viruses were exposed and eliminated will come to light in subsequent chapters. It took many years and several relational losses to bring these to the surface, in order for them to be dealt with.

It seemed trouble and accusations were in hot pursuit of Yvette's life. She was misunderstood and like that old Jamaican proverb says, "Every weh yuh tun macka juk yuh." ("Everywhere you turn prickles hurt you"), no place was safe for Yvette. Oh, she wished death would come and deliver her. "I can't take it anymore. I can't not do anything right. I wish I was not born. It is better to be dead than alive."

With that frame of mind, Yvette saw a bottle on the dresser with pink pills which she thought would do the job. They were large pills. Yvette decided to take a number of them and wait to die but her waiting was in vain. She had not even succeeded in death. There was no hospitalization or sickness.

Yvette now believes those pills might have been vitamins tablets, and not anything to give her the intended overdose she was seeking. No one knew of her suicide attempt. It remained that way for many years until Yvette broke her silence. Her mom however knew she had a troubled child.

The thought of suicide became Yvette's escape route whenever she got into trouble.

At the age of 14, Yvette gave her heart to the Lord and became a Christian but problems and misunderstanding still prevailed at home. Thoughts of suicide continued to plague her mind. Oh how she wrestled with knowing it was wrong! Again at age 15, she almost gave in. This time, she had some brown pills, either sleeping or iron pills, in one hand and the Bible in the other, wrestling with the idea of suicide.

In the end, Yvette didn't give in. Three years later at the age of eighteen, she was delivered from suicidal tendencies but in times of trouble, Yvette still calls on Mr. Death to come knocking on her door. It seems he will not come until her work on earth is over, and her purpose is accomplished.

CONSOLATION AND CHALLENGE

Beloved, as you close this chapter, perhaps Yvette's experience is a reflection of your experience. Perhaps you can identify with some of these viruses and patterns of thinking. I want you to know that there is hope. You are not alone and change is possible. Once we can identify or diagnose the root causes of destructive behaviour, change is possible. More often than not, a prescription is available. The best prescription lies in the truth. Knowing the truth will set you free.

Perhaps you are the parent and you are not even aware of the damage you are doing to your child. Nevertheless, the same prescription is applicable. If you discover the root issues underlying your behaviour, change is possible. The change which eventually came for Yvette and her mother can become your reality too.

If you are struggling with feelings of suicide contact Choose Life International in Jamaica at www.choselifeintl.org or call 876-920-7924 or 876-856-2966.

4.

MAX's SURPRISE

"A real friend is one who walks in when the rest of the world walks out." —Walter Winchell

It should have been a typical Saturday evening when Yvette would have been surfing the internet, checking emails, watching various things on YouTube, and engaging in conversation with friends on Skype and Facebook before retiring for the night. Her friend Blossom appeared on Skype at about 7:30p.m and they talked, catching up on recent events. Blossom inquired about how things were going with Max, Yvette's fiancé.

Yvette shared some of her concerns and Blossom encouraged her not to over-analyse but to let things unfold naturally. While talking to Blossom, Yvette checked her email. One was there from Max. It had a newsletter attached. He had sent it to two other people and copied it to Yvette. Yvette read the newsletter and could hardly speak because the contents of the report immediately started to turn her world upside down. Max had news; news that pertained directly to their relationship and it was not an order for some wonderful item for their wedding. Max had made a life-altering decision and rather than discussing the matter with Yvette, he chose to communicate his decision to significant others first and merely copied her. Max's action seemed disrespectful. Yvette would never have believed that she would be informed of a decision like this in a newsletter.

This was unbelievable! This action signalled clearly to her that she could not possibly have a future with him. Blossom was still online and Yvette shared the contents of the newsletter. Blossom was furious! Yvette, still in shock, felt she needed to get off the call. They ended their conversation around 8:37p.m.

Now, in the quiet, alone, Yvette found herself shouting into the stillness, "I hate you Max! I hate you! And I hate you God, for doing this to me!" She fired off a text message back to Blossom, "I hate him! I hate him! I hate him!"

As soon as the words were out, Yvette realised what she was saying. She was surprised, shocked and scared by her outburst. Never in her life, in all her trials had she ever responded like this! She thought, "Am I doing what even Job did not do in all his trials? Am I cursing God, the One who has been my rock for all these years?" Yvette began sobbing uncontrollably, a part of her fearing that her land-lady might hear her, but partially not caring. It felt like her heart was coming out of her chest and she could not hold back the tears.

As she sobbed, the pain became physical. Her arm and shoulder were aching severely. Her fear became the most tangible thing she was feeling. In terror, she began pleading to God for mercy. "I am sorry God! I don't mean it! I don't mean those words." Yvette tried to peer into the darkness as if to see His face. "But why, why, why, why must I en-dure all this pain?"

It seemed like the night would never end and her tears flowed, enough to fill an ocean. Several hours passed and the pain continued. Yvette began to plead, "Oh God, can't you take me home?" she whimpered, no longer defiant, her passion spent. "I can't do this anymore. Oh God, let me die!"

Yvette pleaded for death in a way she could not recall doing for a long time but she sensed that her pleadings were falling on deaf ears. She knew that her purpose was not yet finished. She felt repentance rise, "Please forgive me, Lord. I know I can't die now, Lord. It would devastate my mentees. Your strength is made perfect in my weakness. So, strengthen me, Lord."

In Yvette's mind's eye, she envisioned her friends and family mourning her death in despair. She felt badly as she was well aware of how sudden death negatively impacts people.

"I don't even have a will," she thought. "Besides, my house needs some cleaning and people can't find me dead with the house like this!" Ridiculous though that thought was, it helped her shake off some of the distress. She told the Lord, "But I am tired of the heartaches and pain."

The physical pain now had her full attention and kept her awake. The agony in her chest continued. Alone and in the dark, all she could do was cry out, "Jesus! Jesus! Jesus!"

Her chest and heart ached so intensely that she wondered if her lung had collapsed again (it had happened twice before) or was this a heart attack? "Oh God, help me!" Her mind screamed as she whispered frantically into the dark. She desperately tried to talk to God, "I never meant the outburst, God! I never meant that! Please forgive me. I want to make heaven my home." The physical and emotional pain was excruciating!

Mercifully, after several hours, sleep came to her rescue. She fell asleep echoing repeatedly, the one name on her mind, "Jesus, Jesus, Jesus."

Yvette did not sleep for long. By 2a.m. she was awake again and the crying resumed. She felt like a mass was sitting on her chest. She went to look in the mirror and panicked. She remembered someone sharing that trauma can lead to cancer. She was envisioning lung cancer being mindful of her previous two lung collapses.

It was then she dragged herself to the desk and flipped open the laptop. She went online and contacted her friends Debbie and Jasmine. She told them to pray for her as she really had no more desire to live. She was facing the dark night of her soul and needed help.

Yvette was petrified at the feeling of alienation from God! She had experienced pain and heartache before but this night she had sunk to a new place of distance and despair. She was riveted on this thought, "Would my faith survive this heartache? It has to!" she thought desperately. "It has to! I don't have anything else to cling to. Would God forgive me for my outburst?" she wondered. "Have I committed the unpardonable sin?"

Several hours later, in the wee hours of the morning, Yvette realized that she was still there. The pain had subsided somewhat. She thought to herself that since God did not let her die, she needed to get her act together. Yvette let her mind return to what had plunged her into this dark place: Max –self-centred, hurtful and clueless. Yvette, hurt again.

Despite this hurt, Yvette made a decision to forgive Max. She desperately wanted God's touch. She recalled a dream she had several years before, in which Jesus refused to touch her because she did not want to forgive another man who had hurt her. In that dream, she eventually chose to forgive and Jesus hesitated ... then touched her. Yvette never forgot that dream and for her, extending forgiveness to anyone has not been an option since that time.

Indeed, the writing on the wall was clear. It was time to let Max go. A Scripture immediately leaped into her mind: "It's better to enter heaven lame than enter hell whole," (Matt. 18:18). She knew then she needed to release Max for the sake of her health and her salvation. Many hours later on that fateful Sunday, she wrote Max a goodbye letter and almost immediately, she began experiencing relief from the physical pains she had been experiencing.

Fortunately, several months prior to this episode, Yvette had established an accountability group of wise counsellors and a social support system which included Pops and Blossom. The next day was Sunday, and Yvette reached out to Pops. In his response, Pops wrote a prayer with prophetic elements and emailed it to her. Below is Pop's response and prayer. In the ensuing years, Pop's prayer was wonderfully answered.

> Oh Lord! What happen now? This young man seems to be trying to destroy you!! Thanks be to God who gives you the **VICTORY!!!!!** Father in heaven, you are Yvette's loving Father who cares for her more than she ever knows. Deliver her from this relationship, oh God, as it has caused her such pain and seems designed to derail and distract her from the ministry and mission you have called her to! Flood her life with

your love, Oh God, giving her the strength and support she needs at this time. Thank you for your peace, grace, love, HOPE and Shalom! Please give her full and complete release from this and bring her to a HIGHER level of faith and trust in you BECAUSE of this long dark night of the soul, as she calls it.

Fill her with your Spirit! Empower her to minister to others through this. Empower her to live FULLY and COMPLETELY in the Christ-life, as she moves forward in you. Give her the WILL and the WAY to forgive Max! But help her to fully let go and to move on with her life, with the power and beauty that only you can give her! And Father, please LOVE on her, especially as she needs you now more than ever. Turn her mourning into dancing.

Weeping may endure for a night but JOY cometh in the morning! Let that SING in her ears, and the sweet songs of a Father's love - her Heavenly Father. Give her your sweet kisses of grace; extra grace oh God, and I thank you in Jesus' name. Amen. Love, peace, grace, hope and God's Shalom!"

Pops

5.

FAULTY FAMILY
FOUNDATIONS

"The most important thing in the world is family and
love." –John Wooden

Family foundations are very significant. When build-
ing an actual edifice, if the foundation is weak or
faulty, the superstructure will be out of alignment
and subject to collapse under the weight it was built to
carry. If the foundations of our lives are poor, especially

the structure of the family, things are likely to go wrong in the lives of those born out of those situations. This is exactly what had happened to Yvette and her parents. Their family foundations were faulty, and Yvette had inherited a cycle of parental rejection that took her over twenty years to unravel.

One of Yvette's mentors, Dr. Donovan Thomas of Choose Life International, once said: "The mother is very often the trigger for teen suicide in the Caribbean." In Yvette's case, it was so. This was compounded by the absence of her father for most of her life. Despite her many scholastic and ministry achievements, Yvette suffered from this deep-seated feeling of being unwanted and unloved. It was while she was on a mission trip in Namibia and Zambia in 2013, that the root of these negative emotions was finally exposed.

She discovered that her mom was an unwanted child, the product of a relationship that went sour, and Yvette, too, was the unwanted product of a relationship that went sour. In Yvette's formative years, her mom was only occasionally part of her life. After age five, she no longer had any contact with her dad, except for about three years after he migrated to another part of the world.

THE FATHER WOUND

As I analyzed Yvette's formative years, I realize she had changed residence three times by the time she was ten years old. Finally, at the age of ten she started living with her mother and resided with her for seventeen years.

For many years as a teenager, Yvette would tearfully sing a popular song by the group Acapella, with lines as follows:

Where is my father?
Why has he gone away?
Why can't he always be here to stay?
Where is my father?
Does he still care?
I need a father who's always there...

Yvette always wondered why her father's involvement in her life was so sparse. After a while, she unconsciously estranged him from her life. This resulted in a 20-year gap of no physical contact and more than ten (10) years without a single conversation. But reconciliation was coming.

Shortly before she reconciled with her dad, her pastor had asked, "Yvette, how come I never hear you talk about your father?" Yvette retorted: "What's there to talk about?" In hindsight, God was using her pastor to prepare her mind for reconciliation with her dad.

Soon after, Yvette received a Facebook message from one of her uncles asking her to contact her dad. She was surprised and sceptical but eventually contacted him by phone. In that conversation she was not sure what to call him. Surprisingly, they had a pleasant conversation in which he told her his thoughts were never far from her despite their estrangement. In that same year, at the age of 32, in the wake of her paternal grandmother's death and her subsequent visit to the USA, Yvette received answers to the questions raised in that Acapella song. Her dad asked her to spend an evening with him before she returned home and Yvette obliged him. That night, he explained it all and at last she finally understood.

Yvette's dad confessed their alienation had to do with the events surrounding the death of Aunt Merl when Yvette was five years old. He blamed her for the death of Aunt Merl, who was closer to him than his real mom. Her connection to that event had unfortunately damaged their relationship.

Nevertheless, Yvette's dad admitted how foolish it was to hold a child responsible in such a situation. But that is what had happened. As her dad shared, Yvette made a decision to forgive. She thought, "None of us can change the past but we can make decisions about the future." Yvette discovered, too, her father had also suffered from faulty family foundations. He never knew his dad.

That evening when she made peace and reconciled with her dad, a hole in her heart was filled and she experienced an indescribable joy. Yvette felt a sense of wholeness because she had always been searching for the love of her biological father in the many spiritual fathers she had embraced over the years

6.

PSYCHOSOCIAL ANALYSIS

"You are loved, prized and valued."
−Courtney Richards

As a student at the Jamaica Theological Seminary, I did several courses including Introduction to Psychology and Developmental Psychology. These courses gave me insight into the causes of Yvette's emotional problems. According to Eric Erickson, in his "Psychosocial Stages of Development," during infancy, a child develops trust or mistrust in the first year of his or her life depending on needs met in his or her social relationships. This would be primarily dependent on the nature of the relationship between child and parents, especially the mother. As a toddler, at age two, autonomy or doubt and fear will be formed depending on how the child is treated as the toddler strives to learn independence and self-confidence.

As a pre-schooler, ages three to five, the child develops initiative or guilt in seeking to initiate tasks and grapple with self-control. In the elementary stage at the age of six, competency or inferiority is developed as the child learns either to feel effective or inadequate. During adolescence or the teen years, the child forms identity or suffers from role confusion, as the teenager works at developing a sense of self, and in young adulthood, ages 20-40, it's either intimacy or isolation as the young adult struggles to form close relationships and to gain capacity for love.

I will stop here since Yvette is not yet 40 years old. This information is widely known and easy to find. You can do a quick internet search to find out about yourself if you are over 40 years old.

Erickson might have well used Yvette as an object for his lesson on the negative side as she was a classic case study. Yvette had developed many of the negative tendencies because her family foundations were faulty. She developed mistrust instead of trust; doubt and fear as autonomy was stifled and independence deterred and guilt had set in. Instead of competence, she developed an inferiority complex and during her teen years, she was definitely confused and her identity formation was delayed.

As a young adult, she struggled greatly to establish intimacy and ended up feeling intensely isolated. Yvette embodied the negative expression of all those stages: such as avoiding relationships in the early years; being suspicious and closely guarded; an unhappy loner; had poor eye contact; procrastinated; had trouble making decisions; was easily influenced; embarrassed when complimented; got depressed easily; was self-deprecatory; had a slumped posture and low energy level; was timid, somewhat withdrawn, overly obedient and questioned her own ability; lacked confidence; found it easy to reject rather than accept herself; sabotaged relationships, practiced avoidant, defensive, self-defeating behaviours and questioned job performance.

Had her foundations been right, she would have stood a good chance of manifesting more of the following positive expressions: invests in relationship, lets mother go, welcomes touching, good eye contact, shares self, independent, not easily led, resists being dominated, able to stand on own two feet, works well alone or with others, assertive when necessary, is a self-starter, accepts challenges, assumes leadership roles, sets goals and goes after them; moves easily and freely with body, wonders how things work, finishes what is started, likes projects, enjoys learning and experimenting; plans for the future, challenges adult authority where appropriate, tends to be self-accepting, maintains friendships, physical and emotional intimacy, participation in games and groups, open and willing to interact and able to make and keep commitments.

As I look at this list of positive expressions, I realize that Yvette was not completely hopeless. She did embody some of these positive expressions as these were her personal goals in her quest to overcome the negatives. It has been a lengthy process, taking many years, but now Yvette manifests more of these positive expressions with a fair degree of consistency. The negatives do rear their ugly heads from time to time. However, Yvette does battle with them to prevent them from dominating her like they did in the past.

I trust by now you have seen the value of good family foundations. This is important for the development of a child and by extension for the development of a healthy society. This psychosocial analysis is not intended to excuse any negative behaviour and assign blame. It is to help you get to the root of your own behaviour and to prevent unnecessary heartache in the future.

A SPIRITUAL FATHER'S BLESSING

It seems that in Yvette's quest for enduring relationships with men, she was seeking the affirmation of her father from whom she was estranged all those years. She needed the love and affirmation of her real father. Yvette needed his blessing. But God has a way of making provisions to recover losses. It was her spiritual father (Pops) who eventually pronounced a blessing on her. In one sentence of affirmation, he had diagnosed and prescribed what she had been searching for all those years. This is what he said to Yvette:

> You are LOVED, PRIZED and VALUED! May God's favour continually rest upon you. Blessings my daughter, keep strong in the Lord and in the power of His might!
> Pops."

At the time, Yvette seriously wondered if Pops had any idea what he had done. She suspected as a Christian Psychologist he was aware but was not convinced he understood the full impact of his blessing. It would completely change her life. When he wrote those words in capital letters (LOVED, PRIZED, VALUED), the scales fell off her eyes. These things were not new to her. They were all over the pages of scripture but yet she had not received them. Why then did she not receive them? Why was Yvette searching all those years for that which she already had? She asked Pops those very same questions. Below is the dialogue that took place via a series of emails.

> Pops!!!!!!!!!! You have no idea what you have done!!!!!!!!!!!!!!!!!!! I bless God for you!!! You have hit the nail on the head by God's Spirit and exciting things are in store!!!!! "You are LOVED, PRIZED and VALUED!" What a word in season! What a word for a generation of hurting women!!! What a

word of hope! What a word of diagnosis and healing. My God is awesome!!!!!!!!!!!!!!!!!!!! You will soon know what I mean Pops!!! Sufficient to say just now, thanks!!!!!!!!!!!!!!!!!!!!!!!!! You should have added and "You are beautiful!!" I have posted these words in my house since you said them.

I am loved.
I am prized.
I am valued.
I am beautiful.

Why do we search for that which already is? Why are we so blind to things God has already given us? How can we be so blind?

Warm Regards
Yvette

Pops had a wise and profound response.
Wow! Praise God my BEAUTIFUL daughter. We search for what we already have because "the blessing has to be BESTOWED before it is OWNED"!! And it's our fathers who should bestow it as the PRIEST in the home! And so, we as both males and females search for what we already have but long for... our father's blessing and that's

why it pains so much when men hurt women, and
when fathers hurt their children.

I BLESS you then BEAUTIFUL daughter of
ZION!! God's charming PRINCESS!!!

Love, grace, and greater beauty!
Pops

Pops is such a wise man and there is a lesson here for
all of us. The father's blessing is important. No wonder Jacob and his mother connived to steal the blessing that
Esau, the older brother was to receive from Isaac his father, before Isaac's death. The story is recorded in the
Bible in the book of Genesis for a reason. The blessing
needs to be bestowed. And I must hasten to say that single
parenting is not God's ideal. As you have seen in Yvette's
history, the absence, especially of a father, often creates
havoc in the child's life and almost automatically impacts
future generations adversely, unless reversed.

CONSOLATION AND CHALLENGE

Beloved, I urge you to take the role of parenting seriously,
if you are a parent. There is so much more to parenting
than making material provisions for the child. There has
to be provision for the emotional needs or the consequences could be dire. The words we speak, especially in

moments of anger, are important. They can be detrimental to your child's well-being as can be seen from Yvette's story.

If you are a young adult or teenager, think carefully about your sexual practices and the consequences of unwanted pregnancies. Think carefully about family foundations. It is not just about having a child. If you are a child reading this book and you have been similarly hurt, I want to tell you that there is hope. Yvette's life has changed and yours can, too. Beloved, as you read this book, remember the words Pops said to Yvette: *you are loved, prized and valued beyond measure.*

7.

TURNING POINT

When the music changes, so does the dance –African Proverb

Don had picked up instantaneously that Yvette was vulnerable and weak. He was a predator and she was easy prey. The Art Room was their primary meeting place. In those meetings, Don had only one thing on his mind: sex, and with each rendezvous he was inching closer and closer to his goal. He made this very clear from their first meeting when things were immediately physical.

As Don was inching closer to his goal, a battle began to rage inside Yvette. How could she be this easy? What about her Christian beliefs? Don himself was a professed Christian from the Pentecostal background.

In retrospect, there was not only a war being waged for Yvette's body but also her soul and her destiny. If God did not intervene, Don would have led her on a path of destruction and she may have turned her back on God. Yvette is forever grateful for God's intervention.

One night, in one of their Art Room encounters, the measure of their emotions was magnified and they both wanted more than kissing. Don's sexual history was of no special interest and thoughts about pregnancy or sexually transmitted diseases were furthest from Yvette's mind. This was the night they would go all the way. With passionate flames burning bright, Don and Yvette engaged in deep kissing. Her blouse was removed and they were about to change position from standing to lying on the floor.

As Don attempted to put Yvette on the floor, suddenly a loud, stern voice (seemingly coming from Yvette, but with such force she could hardly believe it) shouted: "Stop! You are going to be a missionary and you cannot fool around." Yvette was frightened and brought back instantly to her senses. She was not sure what happened to Don but he too stopped and nothing further took place. That evening, he accompanied her to the bus stop like a good gentleman and they talked about what happened and her dream of becoming a missionary. He listened as Yvette spoke, but his replies were laconic.

THE NEW DIRECTION

After ending her escapade with Don, there was a turning point in Yvette's Christian walk. During her relational episode with Don, she battled low self-worth, guilt and shame. She daily asked the Lord to take her life. When He did not, she thought on many occasions of walking in the middle of the road, hoping to be hit by a car.

God, of course had other plans and He paid no attention to the angry question which Yvette daily posed to Him. "Weh yuh wake me up fa?" ("Why did you wake me?"). She was angry with God but even more so at herself for her failures as a Christian.

Eventually, God sent a young man named David to her rescue. He was a committed Christian and he invited her to attend meetings at his church. He was part of the Charismatic movement. Yvette had become somewhat transparent with David and he warned her to be careful of men and not to be so trusting of them.

Yvette accepted his invitation to church. This setting was completely new to her and she was fascinated. One night, at one of those meetings, a lady prophesied over her life and her words became forever etched in Yvette's mind. She said the following:

God is about to remove your timidity. He is about to launch you into something new. God says to tell you to get more of His Word as He is going to use you. The devil has set a trap for you with men. There will be men pursuing but God will deliver you. You are fearful of marriage. I see that you do not want to get married but you will one day get married.

Yvette was shocked. She was right about her timidity and marriage. At times she definitely did not want to be married because of the bad examples she had seen in her family. She was extremely timid and reticent, completely afraid to speak in public. She felt alone and out of place even among friends.

This lady and other prophets informed her that even this loneliness was for her protection, and that God had a hand in that situation. They prophesied about her going to the nations, getting excellent grades in school and that God would send her mentors along the way. One prophesied about a mantle of divine favour resting upon Yvette and God would use her like Joyce Meyer and other powerful women. The main prophet at the time called her a "champion" and told her to learn to think big and enlarge the borders of her mind. He said her thinking was too small.

SPIRITUAL GROWTH

After this, Yvette began reading the Bible and other Christian literature frequently. One day while reading a book titled, *Victory Over the Darkness* by Neil T. Anderson, which addressed issues of inferiority and our identity in Christ, something mysterious happened, and the stronghold of suicide was broken from Yvette's life. Yvette literally felt like a weight lifted from her as she read the book and her countenance changed. She felt light and happy.

What had not occurred by mere fasting and prayer was accomplished through the renewing of her mind. The book answered questions about identity and purpose such as: Who am I? Why am I here? In it, Yvette learned that she was a child of God, inferior to no one. She had been chosen and appointed by God to bear much fruit. In Christ, she was forgiven and set free. She was chosen of God, holy and dearly loved.

MINISTRY INVOLVEMENT

Following her deliverance, Yvette developed a love for prayer. She joined prayer networks and later enrolled at the Jamaica Theological Seminary to be equipped for ministry. Yvette graduated from the Seminary with First Class

Honours. Shortly after, she pursued Graduate Studies and again graduated with honours.

Today, she is super-excited about life. She actively pursues her mission and purpose, is a best-selling author, speaks monthly in churches across Jamaica and has spoken in 14 countries around the world, including churches in Cuba, Haiti, Zambia, Namibia, South Africa, Uganda, Turks and Caicos Islands, Curacao and other countries.

Yvette is blown away by her transformation. Many people who see her boldly preaching before hundreds, month after month, have no idea what a change God has made in her life. Look what the Lord has done!

CONSOLATION AND CHALLENGE

Beloved, I want you to realize that your Creator loves you and has wonderful plans for your life. No matter how dim and dark things seem in your life right now, change is possible. "The thief comes to steal, kill and destroy..." (John 10:10). Your Creator wants to give you life and life in abundance.

If you are a Christian, I want you to realize failure as a Christian does not cause God to love you less, and success does not cause Him to love you more because according to Romans 5, while you were a sinner, Christ Jesus died for you. His love is constant.

Beloved, there is greatness inside you waiting to be released. With the right people and environment, and exercising courage, that greatness can be manifested.

PART II:

BECOMING UNSHACKLED

8.

QUEST FOR FREEDOM

"Freedom cannot be bestowed — it must be achieved." —Elbert Hubbard

W e cannot experience wholeness unless we are emotionally healthy. Emotional well-being has been one of Yvette's chief goals in life. In reviewing her journal entries, she found this goal written repeatedly. Here are two examples:

"I am mentally tough and emotionally healthy and I bounce back from adversity."

"I am emotionally healthy and recover quickly from dis-appointments. I mentor others and help them live their dreams."

The process of journaling has been critical in helping her to maintain emotional well-being. In this chapter, I include three journal entries showing her path to emotional health. They capture the ways in which you too can find emotional health and well-being if your emotions are damaged. For Yvette, it was critical to review her past and her formative years.

She looked for the earliest experiences of trauma, identified patterns and resolved to forgive. She replaced the lies of the Enemy with the truth of God's word, the Bible. Our emotions are qualities and soft spots that must be protected with truth. Feelings are not always logical and feelings are not always truth. Our emotions must be girded with the belt of truth for us to be emotionally healthy.

Forgiveness is critical in the whole process as well as identifying the persons with whom you have been angry. In Yvette's case, she identified her mother, father, ex-boy-friends and other relatives.

FORGIVING PARENTS

Yvette's studies in Psychology and observation of the care her sister-in-law displayed for her niece were the tools the Lord used to help her to understand the challenges of parenting. This helped her to forgive her mom, as she was able to somehow empathize with her struggles and forgive her for her parenting mistakes. Not only did Yvette forgive but she chose to publicly honour her mom at church and in a grand celebration for her 50th birthday.

Sometime after, following an extraordinary experience in Namibia, Africa, Yvette travelled to the United States and honoured her dad. She presented him with a citation of a child's blessing. These acts played a significant role on her journey to wholeness.

FORGIVING EXES

Apart from Max, there was one ex-love interest that Yvette needed to forgive: John. Their relationship was an enigma. He was from the United States and had gone to do missions in Europe. It was a very special and perplexing case that still puzzles Yvette to this day.

John and Yvette met in Germany at a Missions Conference and quickly became friends who fell in love with each other. They shared a similar passion: writing, although Yvette had not yet written her first book. He was tall, fairly dark and handsome. Their communication was easy and he looked beyond Yvette's emotional issues.

He wanted to marry Yvette and move to Jamaica. Yvette was extremely excited about their developing relationship when it ended abruptly. John ended their relationship for ministry reasons. He said he no longer had intentions of moving to Jamaica. To say Yvette was devastated and heart-broken would be an understatement!

Once again, she had found a good Christian man and the thing they both loved separated them. Yvette had experienced something similar years before, with a young man named Horace whom she met at the Seminary. For many months, Yvette wondered if she merely got played. How could she have been this stupid? Did she miss God on this one? She vowed never to marry if the Lord did not reconcile them. She was absolutely convinced he was the right man for her.

It took her one year before she could release John. After eight months, he wrote her a letter of apology explaining what was happening to him at that time. He said she should not feel unloved. He did love her but too many things were happening in his life at that time and he may have ruined hers.

At the same time, he was not interested in being in a relationship with her or anyone at that point. He still was not ready. Yvette was happy for the apology at long last but was still disappointed and hurt. She needed to forgive John, and eventually she did.

HEALING FOR DAMAGED EMOTIONS

Healing for damaged emotions does not occur instantaneously. It is a process. Often, we assume that it is a mere spiritual problem and a lack of faith. Deliverance sessions and prayers alone will not suffice. It necessitates mind renewal and continuous exposure to the truth of God's word before you can be set free. Only the truth can set you free.

Yvette learned that it was not lack of faith that had kept her in bondage but deceit and lies brought about by painful experiences. She learned that many times we try to fix the symptoms leaving the problem intact. It is possible to reset a broken leg instantaneously but if we do not take care of it, it will not heal, and if we don't find out what caused the injury, we may be treating the wrong thing.

The following journal entries capture her personal journey of healing for damaged emotions and her state of mind at the time. She captured the summaries of the two books she read on healing damaged emotions.

Entry I: 2012 August 01
Emancipation Day/ Healing Damaged Emotions

I feel free and at peace! Over the past few days at the Pearsons, God has wrought more emotional healing. He is always keeping me one step ahead. Now I am ready for Spain. I have been reading two books: *Healing for Damaged Emotions: Recovering from the Memories that Cause our Pain* by David A. Seamands and *The Six Steps to Emotional Freedom: Breaking through to the Life God Wants You to Live* by David Clarke. Mrs. Pearson recommended two other books.

Since being here and reading, God exposed why I always try to do right and seek approval. Grandma and Mom always wanted everything done perfectly: the clothes and the house had to be spotless or they would scold and throw back the clothes in dirt for you to wash it over... I learned from an early age the need to always do things right or be rebuked. I was never good enough.

When I tried to commit suicide at 13, it was because I thought I could do nothing right and I believed nobody loved me. My work was always reviewed negatively hence the search for acceptance. Healing damaged emotions is a process, it is not instantaneous. Having damaged emotions and emotional problems is not a result of being unspiritual. Damaged emotions leave people with a sense of inferiority, unworthiness and a sense of not belonging. It usually results in four types of destructive behaviours or characteristics:

- Perfectionism
- Super-sensitivity (need for approval, love and affection)
- Inferiority complex (deep sense of unworthiness, anxiety and inadequacy)
- Fearful (fear of failure).

How to Treat

- Face problem squarely (ruthless, moral honesty).
- Accept your responsibility in the matter.
- Ask yourself if you want to be healed.
- Forgive everyone who was involved in the problem.
- Forgive yourself.
- Ask the Holy Spirit to show you what the real problem is and how you need to pray.
- Walk in God's grace and love.

Satan's deadliest weapon is low self-esteem. The effects of which are as follows:

- Paralyzes our potential
- Destroys our dreams
- Ruins our relationships
- Sabotages Christian service.

Self-image is made of three (3) components:

- Sense of belonging or being loved (Acceptance)
- Sense of worth and value (Significance)
- Sense of being competent (I can do this task, I can cope).

Sources of Self-Image

- Outer world (family, friends, society)
- Inner world (failure to love self)
- Satan and his evil forces
- God and His word

The Holy Spirit helps [comes alongside us and takes us over to the other side] us in our weaknesses...continuous action.

Blessings of the Gospel

God loves us not because we are good but because we need His love to be good. Christ our High Priest bore our sins and infirmities, not because we are good but because we need His love and acceptance in order to be good. The Holy Spirit offers His continuous enabling presence and power, not because we are good but because we need Him in order to be good. God works in all our circumstances to create good for us.

Emotional Problem: An ingrained pattern of faulty thinking, unhealthy emotional expression and sinful behaviour which helps you cope with pain and meets your needs, but which actually cripples all your relationships and gives Satan a foothold in your life.

Emotional Health: An ingrained pattern of accurate thinking, healthy emotional expression and godly behaviour that helps you cope with pain and meets your needs, enriches all your relationships and keeps Satan from being effective in your life.

Steps to Healing

- Build a team (accountability partner)
- Expose and weaken your pattern
- Change your mind
- Express your emotions in a healthy way
- Face your unresolved pain and forgive
- Create a new life
- Changing your mind: What happened? What did you think and feel? What was the truth? What was the result? We are emotional creatures (without apology). Jesus expressed his emotions for e.g.

- Anxiety
- Grief
- Anger
- Joy
- Frustration
- Disappointment
- Compassion.

Emotions are not right or wrong. If in doubt express it. It is significant if it lingers for several hours or affects an important relationship whether positively or negatively. Speak the truth in love. Express them in 4 ways:

1. **Express it as soon as possible after the event** (except when you are intensely angry. Take time to simmer down, you can't communicate well when you are enraged). Within 24 hours is a good standard.

2. **Spontaneously:** It is not forced or planned – as you feel it share it (call, email, etc.).

3. **Directly:** express it directly to the person connected with it except if the person would have a violent reaction and physically harm or kill you. Vent or share it with someone else with whom you are close. Deal directly as much as possible.

4. **Express it fully:** Depending on the event, it may take time to fully express your emotion (divorce, death) sometimes it takes months. In marriage or close relationships, it takes time (that is why John waited so long). It is true for difficult and positive emotions. Keep revisiting until it is all fully expressed.

Keep an Emotional Diary

- What happened?
- What did you feel?
- What did you do with your emotions?
- What was the result?

Do not stuff your emotions. Stop hating myself and seeking approval – God loves me and he thinks precious thoughts towards me and so will I. He has extended mercy and grace to me and I will do so to others. I will learn to express my anger and not stuff it or spew it. Each day is a new day to become wiser and better. Forget the past, forge ahead. No more regret or hurt.

Having learned the need to express her emotions and the value of an emotional diary, Yvette used her journal as a space for healing and private therapy. An important step in the process to becoming free is being honest about our thoughts and anger and expressing them appropriately.

Again, Yvette's journal and prayer provided the space for this. She could freely and honestly say what she thought without fretting about the consequences. In that way, she gained clarity and discovered her root issues and gained more freedom. Here's another example from another journal entry.

ENTRY 2: August 5, 2012
Becoming Free

Truth is I am angry! Angry about my father not being there...Angry about all the negative stuff my mother told me...I forgive, but am angry. Is that possible? I've buried my feelings for so long.

Another part of the process is finding meaning and purpose or what Napoleon Hill refers to as "the seed of an equivalent benefit." It's considering how all things did or could work for your good. It's finding things to be grateful for in your experience or the consequence of the experience and resolving to forgive.

ENTRY 3: 2012 August 7:
Reflections on My Childhood and Teen Years

My mother could have aborted me but she did not. She tried to secure a good life for me by sending me to live with my dad's family. My family tried to protect me. Who knows what else may have happened to me given my adventurous nature?

God allowed my mother to be overprotective for a reason. Perhaps I would have been wild, promiscuous and other bad things. I would not have gotten this close to God and He would not have been my anchor.

God's hand has been with me throughout the years. He provided substitute fathers and mothers along the way. He delivered me from problematic and dangerous situations. All in all, while I cannot change the abuse, neglect etc., God has used them to help me become what I am today. I choose to forgive all who wounded me. I hope all those I wounded including parents, father's family, etc., will forgive me.

It is obvious that neither party intentionally set out to be hurtful. Human beings are like that; we all make mistakes. I am not making excuses, but it is time to move on. I cannot change the past.

CONSOLATION AND CHALLENGE

Beloved, the message here is clear. For your own sake, no matter how wicked or painful or terrible an ordeal you have experienced: be it rape, incest, murder, abuse, torture etc., you need to forgive. Forgiveness is central to the healing of the soul and for emotional wellbeing.

Forgiveness releases blessings and charts the victim on the path of success and growth. On the other hand, unforgiveness and resentment imprison the victim, subjecting him or her to mental and emotional torture. Unforgiveness virtually becomes an idol, an omnipresent, invisible god, daily affecting and controlling the victims thought, life and actions.

It does this with the memory of the perpetrator and of the unforgivable episode which perpetually inflicts pain on the victim, long after the episode has taken place. Unforgiveness is the growth killer and invisible tormentor. Therefore, I urge you to forgive. Jesus said: "If you forgive others for their sins, your Father in heaven will also forgive you of your sins. But if you don't forgive others, your Father in heaven will not forgive your sins" (Matthew 6: 14-15).

Beloved, you need to know how to express your emotions positively and how to find the root causes of your emotional upheavals and negative responses. Very often, the roots are related to events in your childhood. Truth is central to remaining emotionally healthy. We must tell ourselves the truth. It is truth that sets us free.

9.

FINDING YOUR IDENTITY

"Know Thyself"
—Socrates

W hen Yvette left Namibia, she went to the USA and learned more about her family history. She told her Aunt of her African adventures and her quest for identity. Yvette's aunt told her that their family is from the Ashanti or Asante tribe in Ghana. Her paternal family has Irish roots. Aunty had done extensive search on her ancestry in previous years. Yvette was happy to hear this.

Most Afro-Jamaicans have Ghanian ancestry, as majority of the slaves that came to Jamaica were from this region in West Africa. Further research reveals the following interesting facts about the Ashanti tribe.

The Ashanti live in central Ghana in the rainforests of West Africa, approximately 150 miles away from the coast. The Ashanti are a major ethnic group of the Akans (Ashanti and Fanti) in Ghana. Ghana is a fairly new nation, barely more than 50 years old, and was previously called the Gold Coast. Much of the modern nation of Ghana was dominated from the late 17th through the late 19th century by a state known as Asante.

Asante was the largest and most powerful of a series of states formed in the forest region of Southern Ghana by people known as the Akan. Among the factors leading the Akan to form states, perhaps the most important was that they were rich in gold.

It is now politically separated into four main parts. Ashanti is in the centre and Kumasi is the capital. The Ashanti are the largest tribe in Ghana and one of the few matrilineal societies in West Africa. The area of Ashanti is 9400 square miles, with a population of about one million.

The Ashanti people have always been known to be fierce fighters. The people of this tribe have a slogan: "If I go forward, I die, if I go backward I die. Better go forward and die."

When the Ashanti tribe was faced with war, they used drums to signal the upcoming battle. The beat of these drums could be heard through the dense forest. The Ashanti have a special handshake, in which you hold your left hand out to shake hands. This comes from the Ashanti's explanation that the left hand holds the shield, and the right hand holds the spears. So, in order to show your trust in someone, you put down your shield and therefore have your left hand free.

To the Ashanti, the family and the mother's clan are most important. A child is said to inherit the father's soul or spirit, and from the mother, a child receives flesh and blood. This relates them more closely to the mother's clan. The Ashanti live in an extended family. The family lives in various homes or huts that are set up around a courtyard. The head of the household is usually the oldest brother that lives there. The elders choose him. He is called either Father or House Father and is obeyed by everyone.[3]

Like a true Ashanti, in the next season of Yvette's life, she will embrace the fighting spirit of the Ashanti warrior: "If I go forward, I die. If I go backward, I die. Better go forward and die."

CONSOLATION AND CHALLENGE

Beloved, my prayer today for you, is that if you do not know yourself, you too, will come to know yourself and experience liberation. May your Creator order the circumstances of your life in a way that will enable you to find yourself and be spared the heartache that results from lack of self- knowledge! I pray that this takes place sooner rather than later.

10.

PREMIUM CLASS PASSENGER

"Of all the traps and pitfalls of life, self- disesteem is
the deadliest and the hardest to overcome"
—Earl Nightingale

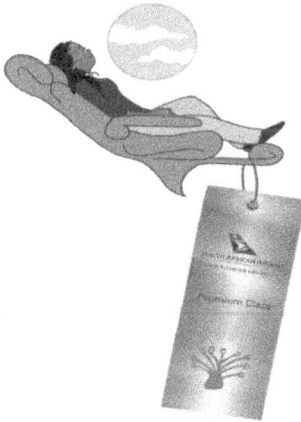

In October 2013, Yvette and her mission partner were
bidding their farewells to Namibia. She thought this
was "goodbye Africa" but four years later, she returned to two different African countries: South Africa and
Uganda. Her first trip on African soil had been an

awesome adventure in Zambia and Namibia and Yvette had learned many lessons.

Although she was looking forward to going home, she had mixed feelings because she missed the loving people she had met. Before returning to Jamaica, Yvette decided to stop over in Florida for a week, during which time she invited her father to her wedding with Max. However, the adventure and lessons for her were apparently not over. God was about to teach Yvette her most vital lesson yet.

Something strange occurred on the first and third flights of this three-part journey to Florida. The departing flight from Namibia was an early one scheduled for 7:15a.m. Yvette arrived at the Windhoek International Airport at about 5a.m. It was a very small airport compared to the airports Yvette had seen over the years.

She and her mission partner Rosie checked in. Prior to boarding the plane, they went to the gift shop and bought some souvenirs. These were their final moments together as a team in Namibia. Their next stop would be the O.R. Tambo Airport in Johannesburg, where they would part company. Rosie would go on to stay in Cape Town, South Africa for another week while Yvette headed to Florida. Together they boarded South African Airways (A Star Alliance Member) Flight 0073. Rosie had already taken her seat in the Coach Class section and Yvette expected to follow suit as they both had purchased H-Coach Class tickets via the same travel agent.

FIRST CLASS EXPERIENCE

As Yvette greeted the flight attendant, she directed her to the front of the plane saying "1C." In Yvette's mind, she had clearly made a mistake. When Yvette searched for 1C, it was right at the front of the plane, in the First-Class section, immediately behind the cockpit! Yvette asked the attendant again for her seating, the attendant smiled and said, "1C" while pointing to the location.

"There must be some mistake," Yvette insisted. She queried a third time, feeling embarrassed, asking a different flight attendant the same question. That attendant asked Yvette to show her the boarding pass and when Yvette did, she confirmed that the seating was right.

In hindsight, they must have thought this woman was crazy. Still in a daze, Yvette went to Rosie and told her what was happening. Rosie told her to just sit and enjoy it and see it as a gift from God. The first flight attendant on seeing that Yvette was still reluctant to take her seat asked if she wanted to change seats and go to the back of the plane instead. In order not to create a scene or further fuss, Yvette heeded Rosie's advice and told her "no." She then took her seat beside a well clad white gentleman.

Most persons would have been glad for such an opportunity but at the time, not Yvette! She knew she had not paid for a First-class ticket and was uncomfortable. In all her 10 years of flying, this was her most uncomfortable flight.

She quickly scanned the section and noticed men professionally clad and began to take note of her own casual attire. She was not shabbily dressed and that eased her mind a bit. Perhaps she should just relax and enjoy the flight. After all this was First Class! She was directly behind the cockpit in the front row. Yvette, however, did not enjoy the premium class treatment that was provided and ate sparingly, being careful to mind matters of etiquette.

In First Class, they were presented with a warm wash towel to clean their hands, and the eating utensils were not made from plastic but were sterling stainless-steel silverware. Honestly, Yvette could not wait for the flight to be over. The flight from Namibia to Jo'Berg was an hour and 45 minutes, but it seemed like forever. Upon exiting, Rosie asked about the experience, but Yvette did not respond with much enthusiasm. Due to her insecurities and poor self-worth, she had not enjoyed the gift that had been provided. Yvette and Rosie then said their goodbyes and headed in opposite directions.

Yvette had a nine-hour layover before heading to Washington D.C. The flight from Jo'Berg to Washington was 18 hours and the adventure was still far from over. God was still trying to get a message across to Yvette about her self-worth which she had not apparently learnt yet. Despite the long flight to Washington, Yvette enjoyed herself. This time she was seated in the Economy class and was treated kindly by her seating companions.

BUSINESS CLASS EXPERIENCE

However, on the third leg of the last flight, she was presented with a similar test as the first flight. Closer to the flight time, the flight attendants did the usual setting up of the boarding area. Yvette saw the rolling of the red carpet and the erection of signs labelled Groups 1-2 and Groups 3-4. Up until then, she had paid no special attention to her boarding pass.

The flight attendants were asking persons with large carry-ons to check them on because the flight was full. The flight was American Airlines Inc - Flight AA 0148. As usual, prior to boarding, First Class and Business Class passengers boarded ahead of other passengers. So Yvette was prepared to wait her turn because she knew she was not in Group 1 or 2. After all, she has just travelled as a coach passenger on the previous flight in congruity with her ticket purchase.

However, when the boarding call was made, Yvette began to panic and have an anxiety attack. Her boarding pass said "Group 1." As the boarding calls continued, she sat there in disbelief and confusion. She thought, "God, not again! What in the world are you trying to do to me? What if I am reading the boarding pass wrong? I'd hate to be embarrassed if I got on that red carpet."

With utmost timidity and trepidation, Yvette entered the red carpet ahead of the majority of passengers who would later board the plane. She asked the very congenial flight attendant if her carry-on was okay or if she needed to check it on. The attendant said, "That's okay. You are in Group 1. Go ahead and board." Yvette was relieved but equally mystified.

This time around, her seating was not in the first section of the plane but in the second section, immediately behind the First-Class curtains. This apparently was Business Class. She was more comfortable here than she was in First Class although quite puzzled by the events that had unfolded.

God clearly was giving Yvette a parting gift, as Rosie had indicated, and trying to get Yvette to see how valuable she was. On arrival at her destination in Florida, Yvette noticed for the first time a golden brown tag on her luggage. It was a South African Airways tag with the label Premium Class. The lesson was now clear.

Yvette was a Premium Class person worthy of being treated with special honour and favour.

She Yvette decided to keep this tag as a symbol of God's favour and an indication that He wanted to bless her more than she could ever imagine. He wanted to take her to a higher place but she was not yet ready by her response to being a Premium Class passenger. No wonder Earl Nightingale remarked:

Of all the traps and pitfalls of life, self- disesteem is the deadliest and the hardest to overcome. For it is a pit designed and dug by our own hands, summed up into the phrase, it's no use, I can't do it. The penalty of succumbing to it is heavy both for the individual, for material rewards lost and for society in gains and progress unachieved.[1]

11.

LOVED, PRIZED AND VALUED

"Don't waste what is holy on people who are unholy.
Don't throw your pearls to pigs! They will trample the
pearls, then turn and attack you."
—Matthew 7:6

People tend to treat us how we see ourselves. As
Yvette reflected on her relational losses and inter-
actions with others, she realized that indeed she
had been selling herself short. She did not know her worth.
This realization made her think of one of the parables of
the kingdom told by Jesus in Matthew about hidden treasure. In Matthew 13:44-46, we read:

> The kingdom of heaven is like treasure hidden in a
> field. When a man found it, he hid it again, and then
> in his joy went and sold all he had and bought that
> field. Again, the kingdom of heaven is like a merchant

looking for fine pearls. When he found one of great value, he went away and sold everything he had and bought it.

Yvette did not see that she was treasure worth sacrificing for. She traded her treasures for trinkets and was satisfied with trinket treatment. Author Marianne Williamson is right in her assessment when she said the following:

> Our deepest fear is not that we are inadequate. Our deepest fear is that we are powerful beyond measure. It is our light, not our darkness that most frightens us. We ask ourselves: "who am I to be brilliant, gorgeous, talented, and fabulous?"Actually, who are you not to be? You are a child of God.[1]

STOP PLAYING SMALL

Williamson further explains: "Your playing small does not serve the world." There is nothing enlightened about shrinking so that other people won't feel insecure around you. We are all meant to shine, as children do. "We were born to make manifest the glory of God that is within us. It's not just in some of us; it's in everyone." And as we let our own light shine, we unconsciously give other people permission to do the same. As we are liberated from our own fear, our presence automatically liberates others.

It took many tragedies for Yvette to see her self-worth and her Pops explained why. He said: "The blessing has to be bestowed before it is owned." A father's blessing affirms the child's identity, self-worth and self-image, and shapes the child's destiny.

Many fathers do not know this. My hope is that men and fathers will read this book and change their behaviour. Being a man is more than being virile or being a sperm donor. If we are to stop the bleeding of the hearts of sons and daughters, men have to change and rise to the occasion. Thank God for spiritual fathers and mentors like Pops who have been standing in the gap for years, helping us to become wiser and better.

CONSOLATION AND CHALLENGE

Beloved daughter of the Most High, receive this blessing as a bestowment from Yvette's Pops to you: "I BLESS you then BEAUTIFUL daughter of ZION!! God's charming PRINCESS!!! You are LOVED, PRIZED and VALUED!"

Beloved son of the Most High, receive this blessing as a bestowment from Yvette's Pops to you: I BLESS you then MIGHTY son of ZION!! God's warrior Prince!!! You are LOVED, PRIZED and VALUED!"

Following Neil Anderson's teaching in Steps to Freedom in Christ, make the following renunciations:

Renounce the lie that you are rejected; unloved, dirty or shameful; in **CHRIST** you are completely accepted.

Renounce the lie that you are guilty, unprotected, alone or abandoned; in **CHRIST** you are totally secure.

Renounce the lie that you are worthless, inadequate, helpless or hopeless; in **CHRIST** you are deeply significant.

May you realize today that you are loved, valued and prized! May you learn from the story of Yvette's life that you are a treasure despite what others think or say or how they treat you! May you begin to value yourself highly and live in that light, so that you can begin to reap the seed sown from this revelation of light! This will cause others, perhaps not in all cases, but more often than not, to treat you with dignity and respect.

Will you renounce the lies of the Enemy of your soul? Will you receive the blessing bestowed by Yvette's spiritual father and your heavenly Father in this book?

May you find liberation from self-hatred and be set free to live! Today is your day to gain victory over the darkness of self-hatred!

12.

LOVE AFFAIR WITH PETER

Then Andrew brought Simon to meet Jesus. Looking intently at Simon, Jesus said:
"Your name is Simon, son of John—but you will be
called Cephas" (which means "Peter").
—John 1:42

I have always admired Peter, affectionately called the
"Rock," by our Lord. Over the years, through the ac-
counts of him given by other writers, I developed an
intense love affair with him. Peter's life also gave Yvette
hope and his teachings were embedded in her heart.

Whenever Yvette thought of giving up, Peter gave her hope!

Through his writings she developed a deep yearning and desire for the return of his King, who also became her King, her provider and her protector. Now that Peter's journey on earth is complete, Yvette feels honoured to tell his story and to share his teachings. May you, like Yvette find comfort and peace from Peter's life and writings! May you find courage to suffer and stand like Peter, even to the very end of your days on earth!

HIS BIRTH AND NATIONALITY

Peter was of Jewish descent; a native of a place called Galilee, a large region in northern Israel. It was the tribal region of Dan and Napthali, two sons of the patriarch Jacob, who is also known as Israel. It was a region where non-Jewish foreigners had settled. Galilee was also the region where Peter's King grew up and the place where the King did mighty miracles. Galilee was said to be the birthplace of philosophers and mystical miracle workers. Despite this reputation, the region was also known for being "a hotbed of political activity and some of it violent - especially in the last few generations of New Testament scholarship."[1]

Peter was a true son of this region, as you will see later in this biographical reflection of his life and he became quite influential in his lifetime. When Peter spoke, others listened and followed suit; and eventually he became an Elder Statesman of the Early Church. Peter had no formal education but became quite successful in business. His was a thriving fishing business and at his core he was an ardent fisherman. His brother Andrew was his business partner and was the crucial link that eventually initiated Peter's meeting with the King. Thanks to his brother, Peter's life was radically transformed and he became one of the King's most loyal subjects. Peter loved the King dearly and although he had a thriving business and a wife to support, when the King asked him to give up his business; he surrendered it all for the love of the King. He became a faithful servant in the business of the King.

CONNECTION TO THE KING

This King was not like other kings. He wore no crown and lived in no palace. He was from another planet, another kingdom not of this world. While He sojourned on earth for 33 and a half years, He amassed no wealth and was dependent monthly on the financial gifts of His faithful followers. Peter also embraced this lifestyle.

The King was a powerful speaker and miracle worker. News of his acts spread far and wide. The religious leaders of the time became exceedingly jealous and conspired to kill him. They succeeded in their plans and the King's earthly sojourn ended at the young age. But this was not the end of the King. In true Galilean style, the King accomplished a mystical feat. He was resurrected from the dead. Upon His reported resurrection, He appeared to Peter and even 500 of his followers simultaneously and in diverse places, in diverse manners, often disguising his true form. But He was not to be on earth for long, even in this resurrected mystical state.

He only stayed for 40 days and then He commissioned His faithful followers, including Peter, to a world-wide mission. They were to preach the Gospel of the Kingdom of God and pass on His teachings beginning at Jerusalem. They were to prepare people throughout the world for His return and warn them of the need to escape the impending judgment which would follow His return.

Peter was a true subject and mentee of the King. People took note that even though Peter had no formal education that he had spent much time with the King. His intimate relationship with the King permeated his life and affected his conduct. Peter's highest aim became that of pleasing his King.

In Peter's latter years, he became a great writer encouraging others to overcome their struggles in service of the King. He spoke from his experiences of failing the king earlier in his early life. Towards the close of Peter's earthly journey, he reflected on his mistakes and was determined to leave a legacy, an eternal reminder for his followers on how to successfully follow the King.

Peter's particular area of expertise in writing was *Suffering and the Christian Faith: How to Overcome Adversities.* After his early failures, he gained strength and courage to endure much suffering for his belief in the King. He was imprisoned and beaten for his faith. He lived in a society hostile to his faith and beliefs and like the King, he would ultimately forfeit his life at the hands of those hostile to his faith and practice.

Some of his countrymen considered Peter a traitor having become a subject of this strange King. He had turned his back on some of the religious practices of his forefathers and his nation. He had embraced non-Jewish people and ate with them in their homes; a practice frowned upon by his fellow Jews. Peter crossed deeply entrenched ethnic and cultural divides and barriers by associating with people of other ethnicity considered to be unclean; even called "dogs" and "outcasts" by some. He became a revolutionary following in the footsteps of his King; performing glorious miracles like Him; even the raising of one from the dead and the miraculous healing of the sick, the lame and the diseased. He even succeeded in a special feat that only His King had ever accomplished: he walked on water.

At first it was a scary experience. Peter panicked and began to sink but the King was with him, and when he cried out for help, the King steadied him and thus Peter walked on water twice. Peter *failed forward* and became fearless. Yvette's greatest admiration of Peter is not for his miracles but his ability to fail forward and withstand suffering. For she, like Peter, has failed the King and the example of how the King dealt with Peter's failure and subsequently used him, gives her eagle's wings to fly and soar above her adversities and her many failures.

13.

PETER'S FAILURES AND SUCCESSES

The third time he said to him, "Simon, son of John, do you love me?" – John 21:17

In Peter's first attempt at public speaking, at least 3000 people were persuaded to become followers of the King. Peter was not interested in speaking about himself; it was all about his gracious King from another place. Peter was the great forerunner of men like D.L. Moody, Smiths Wigglesworth; Charles Spurgeon (prince of preachers); Jonathan Edwards and Billy Graham. His gift for speaking also resulted in his greatest moment of sorrow and regret. Like a true son of Galilee, Peter was sometimes impetuous and hot blooded and he wore his heart and mouth on his sleeves. He was what we call in Jamaica "dry eyed." He spoke of things as he saw and felt them. He would make bold and insightful revelations about significant spiritual truths and then he would say things that warranted a rebuke.

On that fateful night of Peter's greatest moment of sorrow and failure; the King forewarned that His death was near. Peter, in response to this news, boldly declared even if all forsook the King, he would stay with Him and even die for Him. The King, ever so insightful, being fully aware of Peter's motive and intention, knew that when the moment of truth came, Peter would not stand. In fact, when he told this to Peter, he would believe none of it. When the time of testing came, just as the King had predicted, Peter failed to deliver.

On that fateful night when the security forces came to arrest the King, Peter who had a violent tendency, cut off piece of the ear of one of the members of the security forces. It is rumoured Peter had really intended to go for the neck but had missed. The King rebuked Peter for his action and performed a miracle to restore the soldier's ear to its former state. It was then that Peter's boldness began to fade. The King went quietly with the security forces and Peter and John, another follower who greatly loved the King, followed closely behind. As they remained in the shadows, but within sighting distance of Him, they saw that the King was subjected to a flagrantly dishonest trial system and subsequent torture.

At three different points, Peter was asked if he knew the King, and fear got the better of him. He denied knowing the King all three times. On one occasion, being the third, the King even heard him and looked at him. In that moment, Peter was filled with such deep agonizing sorrow and pain that he wept bitterly and temporarily lost his faith. This was the nadir of Peter's life: he had denied his King and he did not have the strength to get back up again. But the King was not through with Peter. His plans for Peter's life had not ended. Upon his resurrection from the dead, He paid Peter a glorious visit.

THE KING RETURNS

After the King's death, Peter went back to his fishing business along with other followers of the King. One early morn after Peter had toiled all night with his friends but had caught no fish; the King came in disguise and told them where to fish. It was reminiscent of a similar event that happened during the early days when the King was just gathering His chosen ones. Peter and his friends obeyed the stranger and caught so many fish that they were unable to haul in the net. In that glorious moment with such a great catch and the promise of business success, Peter realized that the man who had instructed them to "throw their nets over to the other side" was his King in disguise.

Peter was horrified, still filled with shame and guilt at the memory of his denial and could scarcely face the King. His friend and business partner John, whispered in his ear, "It's the King." Totally un-alarmed by their actions, the King told them to bring Him some of their catch. Peter climbed back into the boat and dragged the net ashore. It was full of large fish but even with so many the net was not torn. The King said to them: "Come and have breakfast." None of the followers dared ask Him, "Who are you?" They knew it was the King. The King came, took the bread and gave it to them and did the same with the fish. This was the third time that He had appeared to His followers after He was raised from the dead. Now, the King was about to do a special act for Peter despite his denial. Peter, however, had no clue. He was expecting judgment not mercy and grace or a commission to pursue for the rest of his earthly life.

PETER'S REINSTATEMENT

This is how the King accomplished this gracious, mind boggling, forgiving, awesome feat! When they had finished eating, the King said to Peter:

> "Simon, son of John, do you love me more than these?"
> "Yes, Lord," Peter answered, "you know that I love

you."

The King said, "Feed my lambs."

Again the King said, "Simon, son of John, do you love me?"

He answered, "Yes, Lord, you know that I love you."

The King said, "Take care of my sheep."

The third time he said to him, "Simon, son of John, do you love me?"

Peter was hurt because the King asked him the third time, "Do you love me?" He said, "Lord, you know all things; you know that I love you." The King said, "Feed my sheep.

"Very truly I tell you, when you were younger you dressed yourself and went where you wanted; but when you are old you will stretch out your hands, and someone else will dress you and lead you where you do not want to go." The King said this to indicate the kind of death by which Peter would bring Him glory! Then he said to him, "Follow me!"

Peter turned and saw that John, another disciple whom the King had greatly loved, following them as they had their talk. John was the one who had leaned back against the King at the supper when the King announced his impending arrest and subsequent betrayal and had said, "Lord, who is going to betray you?"

When Peter saw him, he asked, "Lord, what about him?" The King replied, "If I want him to remain alive until I return, what is that to you? You must follow me." Because of this, a rumour spread among the followers of the King that John would not die. But the King did not say that he would not die; He only said, "If I want him to remain alive until I return, what is that to you?"[2]

The point is the King did not want Peter to focus on the call of another but on his own mission and purpose. After this glorious reinstatement, Peter left the fishing business for good and returned to the service of his King and remained faithful even unto death, dying almost in like manner as his King. He subsequently developed an international following, spreading the King's teachings far and wide.

PETER'S DEATH

Peter had eventually lived up to his name and became a rock! According to tradition, he suffered martyrdom under Nero in 68 A.D. He was crucified upside down as he did not think he was worthy to die exactly like his King. It was an expression of sorrow and humility for having denied the King, prior to the King's death. With his brother, Apostle Paul, he finished his course and passed on from earthly to heavenly things.[3]

Yvette and I want to be like Peter: failing forward, rising from defeat and remaining faithful to the King even in death. He is a strange King to follow but like Peter and many others, we believe wholeheartedly in Him and we are looking forward to His glorious return.

PART III:

BECOMING WHOLE

14.

OVERCOMING HEARTBREAK

"He heals the broken-hearted and bandages their wounds." –Psalm 147:3

Yvette's experience with suffering and heartache led me to study the subject of faith, suffering and success. I wanted to know what made some people stand while others succumbed. I wanted to know if it were possible to recover from heartbreak and become whole again.

I looked at suffering through the eyes of those who endured; both Christian and non-Christians. What is it that makes some people triumph in suffering while others are defeated by it? Peter was an excellent model of one who not only experienced tremendous suffering unto death but ultimately thrived after moments of failure.

Peter also taught others how to overcome suffering and heartbreak and I want to do the same. My personal life goal is to finish my course well with joy and maintain my faith regardless of the pressures of life. It is to come out as pure gold like Peter. This goal is captured in my life verse found in Acts 20:24: "But none of these things move me; nor do I count my life dear to myself, so that I may finish my race with joy and the ministry which I received from the Lord Jesus, to testify to the Gospel of the grace of God."

The original recipients of Peter's letters were suffering because they were followers of the King. This was during Nero's persecution in AD 64-68. His advice to them over two millennia ago is still applicable today. This advice transcends era, religion and culture if you know how to wisely apply it.

I love the concept of endurance so evident in his letters. As Peter's sojourn on earth was coming to a close, with the help of his friend Silvanus, he left a written legacy (two letters) for his followers to learn to suffer and stand and avoid deception. These letters were helpful in aiding me to overcome my dark nights. Peter is one of my symbols of hope.

I could not write a book about overcoming heartbreak and not include anything about him.

In 2 Peter 1: 3-4, we learn that God's divine power has given us everything we need for life and godliness through our knowledge of Him (Jesus) who called us by His own glory and goodness. Through these He has given us His very great and precious promises, so that through them we may participate in the divine nature, and escape the corruption in the world caused by evil desires. These precious promises and provisions are merely to be discovered.

Suffering is the state of undergoing pain, distress, agony or anguish mentally, emotionally or physically; to be subjected to injury, loss or anything unpleasant.[4] Suffering leads to heartbreak and heartache, the emotional pain we feel when we lose someone loved. Peter's letters explore some of the questions we tend to ask in heartbreak which are as follows:

- Is it strange or necessary?
- Is it fair, just and reasonable?
- Is it shameful or dignified?
- Is it common?
- Will it last forever?
- Is there a sure way not to lose our faith?

His followers had similar questions and from his responses to them, I have identified 21 secrets to overcome heartbreak, pain and suffering. Each will be explained in detail throughout the chapter. They are as follows:

1. It's Inevitable
2. Acknowledge the Loss and Give Yourself Time to Grieve
3. This Too Will Pass
4. Find Positive Meaning and Purpose
5. Control Your Attitude and Response
6. Be Joyful
7. Be Thankful and Count Your Blessings
8. Desist from Revenge | Maintain a Pure Conscience
9. Emulate Positive Models and Examples
10. Turn to God
11. Pray
12. Perform Acts of Service
13. Forgive
14. Maintain Identity and Dignity
15. Reach for Social Support
16. Vulnerability and Transparency
17. Exercise Right and Wise Conduct
18. Manage Your Mind
19. Stay Away from Toxicity
20. Exercise Self-Control
21. Have Hope for the Future. Persevere and Turn it into Glory

I have applied these 21 unfailing principles (secrets) on overcoming suffering to my life with tremendous results.

21 BIBLICAL SECRETS TO RECOVER FROM HEARTBREAK AND SUFFERING

Below is a brief summary and explanation of each of the secrets on the aforementioned list.

1. *It's Inevitable*

In dealing with heartbreak and suffering, it is of utmost importance that we have an appropriate assessment of it. Heartbreak and suffering are commonplace experiences of human life from which no human is exempt. If we understand this, we should prepare for it instead of viewing it as a surprise or fussing about it.

Many of us are bewildered by suffering instead of expecting it and seeking ways to cope. Wishing it were otherwise is not helpful and refusing to accept it as part of normal experience is counter-productive. Peter told his suffering followers in 1 Peter 4: 12, "My friends, do not be surprised at the terrible trouble which now comes to test you. Do not think something strange is happening to you."

2. *Acknowledge the Loss and Give Yourself Time to Grieve*

This is an important step in the process of healing. Don't be too quick to move on. This is a recipe for disaster. Rebound relationships are often disastrous. You need time to detox and examine your emotions and deal with the hurt and pain. Don't pretend as if you are fine and not hurting. Acknowledge it. This is the first stage of healing.

Allow yourself to grieve the loss of security and expectations; the loss of hopes and dreams and whatever else the suffering causes. Afterward, begin to take steps to move forward. Take your time. We all don't recover at the same pace. Remember emotional wounds are not healed instantly. There are often multi-layers of pain, and just when you think you have dealt with them all, suddenly something comes up again; something triggers the pain.

In this grieving process, talk to someone you trust and get counselling as Yvette did, if needed. It might not be professional but seek wise counsel from someone competent in the area of loss or suffering. Gaining valuable insights is the key to your healing.

3. This Too Will Pass

Heartbreak is not surprising and neither will it last forever. "This too will pass" is a good standing phrase that captures the temporal nature of suffering. It encourages and strengthens many sufferers. In as much that the rain does not fall every day and in as much as the sun rises and sets, suffering is not interminable. Yvette's YouTube mentor, Les Brown, says it this way, "Whatever you are going through, it has not come to stay, it has come to pass." This problem will not bother you forever. Even humans die.

4. Find Positive Meaning and Purpose

The reason for suffering matters and the meaning we attribute to suffering matters. In 1 Peter 3:13-18, he tells his followers not to think they are cursed because they suffer. They may even suffer for doing right and they are blessed if they suffer for doing right. He tells them that no one can really hurt them if they suffer for doing right. Yes, physically and emotionally they will be hurt but ultimately as followers of the King who love him, the King will work in all things for the good of them that love him and are called according to his purpose (Romans 8:28).

The King will make it pay dividends as Napoleon Hill says: "There is no such thing as an unprofitable experience. Make every circumstance good or bad, pay dividends. Life is a continuous process of education. Learn from all experiences good or bad. Be on the alert for gains of wisdom."[5]

Heartbreak has not ultimately come to kill you but to produce faith or test faithfulness. In 1 Peter 1:6, he explains: "These troubles have come to prove that your faith is pure." He told them in 1 Peter 1:9 that as they stand in suffering they are receiving the goal of their faith, "the salvation of their souls."

Depending on the perspective of the sufferer and the meaning attributed to suffering, the heartbreak can lead to the discovery of one's life purpose. That which breaks our heart is a clue to our purpose. Pain is the flip side of purpose. God comforts us in all our suffering so that we can comfort others with the comfort we have received (2 Corinthian 1:4). It means we are called to help people who suffer similarly to us with the solutions we found to overcome our pain. That's one way of determining your purpose in life.

5. Control Your Attitude and Response

Closely aligned with meaning and purpose are attitude and response. John Maxwell in his book, *The Winning Attitude* coined the catchphrase, "Attitude determines altitude." While we have no control over the majority of the things that will result in our suffering, we have control over our attitude/ response. Jim Rohn in his inimitable style asserts, "It's not what happens that determines your life's future. It is what you do with what happens. All of us are in a little sailboat. It is not the blowing of the wind that determines your destination. It is the set of the sail."[6]

Peter outlines various attitudes and responses we should have in suffering which are also some secrets to recover from heartbreak. They are as follows:

- Rejoice, be joyful (1 Pet. 4: 13)
- Purify body and soul (1 Pet. 2:1)
- Be patient (1 Pet. 2: 20-21)
- Express love and forgiveness (1 Pet. 4:8)

- Bless and curse not (1 Pet. 3: 9-11)
- Show respect (1 Pet. 2:17)
- Maintain a clear conscience (1 Pet. 3:16)
- Refrain from complaining (1 Pet. 4:9)
- Don't pay back wrong for wrong (1 Pet. 3:9)

I will elaborate on some of these which I believe are hardest to do: being joyful, blessing instead of cursing and maintaining a clear conscience. Beloved, our attitude and our response to suffering will determine whether we stand or succumb.

6. Be Joyful

It is natural for us when enduring pain and despair to be unhappy. To ask a sufferer to rejoice seems to be an unreasonable demand. However, if the suffering followers of the King really believed that the King would cause some good to come from their suffering, and focused on the outcome of their suffering, realizing that in suffering they were identifying with the King, indeed their suffering could be counted as joy. If we remember that God makes all things beautiful in his time (Eccl. 3: 12); that those who suffer for the King will share His glory when He returns, certainly there will be cause to rejoice.

If we think of suffering as producing character and patience as part of our training in holiness and maturity, then we can rejoice in it. Peter addressed this in 1 Peter 5:10.

Indeed, we too can have a joyful attitude in suffering if we see some positive outcome as a result of our suffering. Again, Napoleon Hill reminds us that there is "a seed of equivalent benefit in every experience." If we can find it, certainly we will have joy and cause to rejoice.

7. Thanksgiving and Counting Your Blessings

There is another cliché often used in times of suffering that can lead to joy: "count your blessings." If we begin to count our blessings even in heartbreak, we become thankful and our attitude often changes in suffering. It is Nick Vuijic, a man born without arms and legs that said, "I've never seen a thankful person who is bitter or a bitter person who is thankful."[7]

Nick turned his lemons into lemonade. Although he was born without limbs, today he has a ministry called "Life Without Limbs." He is married and has three children. He turned a despairing situation into one of hope. He is making a difference today using the very same thing that once brought him pain and suffering.

8. Desist from Revenge and Maintain a Pure Conscience

As it relates to maintaining a pure conscience, Peter reminded his followers that although suffering is natural, one dare not allow his or her heart to be corrupted by it through malice, hatred, resentment, bitterness and unforgiveness.

There is grave danger in this because these things are detrimental to the life and health of the sufferer in the long run. It is a well noted observation from medical personnel that those who harbour such things, generally end up with a stressful life leading to maladies such as hypertension, heart attack, ulcers, strokes and all kinds of muscular aches and pains. Therefore, Peter warns against this, "Rid yourself of all evil, all lying and hypocrisy" (2 Peter 1:15).

Do bear in mind he was speaking to people who had experienced the loss of their possessions, status, friends and loved ones; some were imprisoned and displaced. Peter himself had endured similar suffering and was leading by example. To endure in suffering should be our goal. As Frank Sinatra said, "The best revenge is massive success." Similarly Beloved, I warn you against developing bitterness, resentment and unforgiveness because of your suffering. In the long run, these attitudes will only prolong and worsen your suffering, not relieve it. These things eventually result in self- destruction. Do not seek revenge. Seek justice and maintain a clear conscience.

9. Emulate Positive Models and Examples

There is nothing so potent as a living example or model to emulate and encourage someone along their journey. Peter used himself as an example. He used Noah as well as other elders and best of all; he pointed the followers to the King's example in suffering. Sufferers are not alone (1 Peter 5:8). In 1 Peter 2:22, we see when the King suffered, he did not sin; there was no guile or retaliation and no threatening. He left all judgment to His God and Father. Peter encouraged these sufferers to cast their care on the One who will make all things right. He encouraged them to be faithful because their faithfulness will be rewarded.

In listening to many teachers of success, modelling is emphasized repeatedly. If you want to be successful, find out what successful people do and do likewise. If you do not want to fail; find out what failures do and avoid doing likewise. Peter was thus giving them a formula for recovering from suffering and being whole. I encourage you today to research and reflect on others who suffered and recovered, then follow their pattern or example.

10. Turn to a Higher Power (God)

There are some sufferings that only God can fix –no friend, no sermon, no spouse, no book and not even our best preparations can help; only the intervention of our Maker and Divine Helper will suffice. Peter encouraged his followers to turn to their Creator and their King in their suffering. "Come to the Lord Jesus, the stone that lives... Anyone who trusts in Him will never be disappointed" (1 Peter 2: 4-7). The latter part of this verse is my favourite Scripture especially in times of great testing. It is one of the great precious promises that have enabled me and others to rise above heartbreak, suffering and adversity. Those who trust the Judge of all the Earth to do right will not be put to shame. It is he who heals the broken-hearted and binds up their wounds (Psalm 147:3).

Peter is careful to point out that many will not embrace the Creator in suffering because Christ is the stone rejected. Beloved, everyone has a choice. I can only respect your choice but I know for those of us, like Peter and his followers, Christ is a pillar of comfort and a pillow of peace to rest in times of suffering. Peter told these sufferers, "A person might have to suffer even when it is unfair but if he thinks of God and can stand the pain, God is pleased..." Peter tells them to think of God so they can withstand the pain of unfair suffering because their God sees and His ears are open the cry of sufferers.

11.   Prayer

As is written in 1 Peter 3:12: "The Lord sees the good people and listens to their prayers. But the Lord is against those who do evil." God sees and hears your cries in your brokenness. He is close to the broken-hearted (Psalm 34) and will ultimately make things right.

Therefore, Peter lists prayer among his fire proof principles to recover from heartbreak and loss. He implores his suffering followers to give all their worries to God because He cares for them (In 1 Peter 5:7). Furthermore,

James another contemporary of Peter tells us, "Is anyone in trouble, let him pray..." (James 5:13).

12.   Perform Acts of Service

Peter encourages his suffering followers to serve each other. It is while Ruth was helping Naomi that her heart was healed; and it is as Naomi helped Ruth (in the book of Ruth) that she went from bitter to pleasant. It is often in losing ourselves that we find ourselves. Of course, not all sufferers are able to serve, as illness may incapacitate them and prevent this from happening. In this case, their state of brokenness often becomes an opportunity for someone else to exercise compassion and carry out acts of service.

In cases where the sufferer is not incapacitated, serving others will bring joy to the sufferer and when the focus is off oneself, hope comes to light. In fact, Peter reminds his followers, "...each of you has received a gift to use to serve others. Be good servants of God's various gifts of grace" (1 Peter 4:8-10). Service should be done as an act of love. Thus, Peter tells them to love each other deeply; to be hospitable, open their homes to each other and forgive others of their many sins.

13.   Forgiveness

Without forgiveness your heart will not be healed. We saw this in Yvette's story. Unforgiveness is like swallowing poison while expecting your perpetrator to die. When one does not forgive, the act of hurt continues to dominate one's thoughts and heart and can lead to serious illness. It eventually destroys the broken one.

Forgiveness does not mean you forget the hurt. It is a decision to release the anger, bitterness and desire to take revenge on your perpetrator. It requires you to acknowledge the hurt and its effect but release the desire to get even.

In time, you will find your feelings changing and the pain reducing. This is why prayer matters. I believe forgiveness is a supernatural act and we have to depend on God to get us through. We cannot do it by ourselves but it is necessary for healing and wholeness.

14.   *Maintain Identity and Dignity*

Human dignity, self-image and self-esteem matter to us all. Even in suffering, these should be maintained. Sufferers often lose their self-esteem and self-image. If the suffering is caused by illness, very often their bodies become frail and beauty and strength fade. Often times, the sufferer stops taking care of him or herself and may be abandoned and abused by others. In such a state, self-esteem, self-image and human dignity are eroded. Peter encourages his suffering followers to remember their identity and whose they are. They are a "peculiar people, a chosen generation, a royal priesthood, a people God called out from darkness into his marvellous light to show forth the praises of the One who called them" (2 Peter 2: 9).

Affirming relationships are important. Yvette had several persons who affirmed her value in her time of brokenness. Her spiritual mentor reminded her that she was a daughter of the King; beautiful, prized, loved and valued. Sufferers who are heartbroken need to be assured of their dignity and esteem. They need affirmation which will enable them to heal and find wholeness again.

15.   *Reach for Social Support*

Do not suffer in silence. Resist the urge to be alone indefinitely. It is so intriguing that the things that enable us to stand are the very things we do not want to do naturally when we are in pain. This is why we need the help of others. The broken-hearted should cry out for help although sometimes they cannot. Sufferers need love and a social support system during their times of suffering. They need a safe place and people they can relate to or reach out to for help. This help can be physical or emotional. I encourage sufferers to initiate the reach for help.

Too many people are suffering silently and prolonging their pain. Yvette learned firsthand that healing comes through community. In *I'm Not Okay and Neither Are You* Dr. Clarke emphasizes *no one heals alone.* I believe this is why Peter encouraged his followers to love each other deeply, open their homes to each other and serve each other. No man is an island and keeping hurt to yourself does not help you or anyone else.

Loving one another also means coming alongside the other and being there to help. Peter placed a great emphasis on love and respect as he addressed his suffering followers. "Show respect for all people: love the brothers and sisters in God's family, respect God and honour the King" (1 Peter 2:17).

Yvette overcame her suffering quicker than normal because she took the initiative to establish her social support group. This greatly aided her healing when the relationship with Max went sour. Too many of us sit passively waiting for someone to offer help. We must be a friend before we need a friend. I can say categorically that your recovery from various heartaches will be faster with support. Beloved, begin to establish a support system. Join a church, get involved in other groups and make friends before you need them.

16.   *Vulnerability and Transparency*

Yvette learnt from the consequences of suffering in silence to be vulnerable and transparent with her life and her struggles. Too many of us on account of privacy don't want anyone to know our pain or weaknesses. Everything is "hush- hush." I really do not believe this kind of secrecy helps anyone.

It only results in silent suffering and prolongs personal pain. David in Psalm 32 says, "When I kept silent, my bones wasted away through my groaning all day long." The Scripture encourages us to confess our faults and weaknesses one to another and pray one for another that we might be healed. I'm not saying entrust yourself to everyone and tell everyone your business. Have one or two people with whom you can be vulnerable and transparent, who will help you in times of need. Even Jesus expressed His sorrow to his friends. When he was facing death, he asked three of his closest disciples to join him in prayer. When they failed to support him, His Heavenly Father sent angels to strengthen Him. We certainly do not need any less support and should follow suit.

17. Exercise Right and Wise Conduct

We should not use heartbreak, suffering and pain as an excuse to sin or behave badly. Peter addressed this in no uncertain terms. "It is God's desire that by doing good you should stop foolish people from saying stupid things about you. Live as free people, but do not use your freedom as an excuse to do evil" (1 Peter 2:15).

Pain can lead to impaired judgment and foolish decisions. How many have committed suicide, become drug addicts, teenage mothers or end up behind bars as a result of bad decisions in the midst of heartache and pain? Hurting people often hurt others. Being mindful of this, Peter encourages his suffering followers to exercise right and wise conduct.

This is why mindset maintenance and self-control are vitally important in preparing for suffering and while we are suffering. We become what we think. "Be careful what you think because your thoughts run your life" (Proverbs 4: 23). We should not use our pain as an excuse to disrespect others. Very often, this is exactly what we do because suffering blinds us. Right thinking leads to right action; wrong thinking leads to wrong behaviour.

In our pain and anger, it is natural to rebel against authority especially if they are the ones inflicting the pain and causing sorrow. I have seen many children rebel in the face of pain inflicted by parents, and in seeking relief and escape, jump from the frying pot into the fire. Their escape method became even more injurious. The stories of many runaways reflect this. Their escape turned out to be greater sorrow resulting in things like unwanted pregnancy, prostitution, a life of crime and violence, hurt and abuse and other maladies.

Another example is in marriage. When pain is experienced in marriage, spouses rebel against each other, committing adultery and acts of infidelity. There is a time to submit and a time to shake off the yoke, and there is a proper place to do so. We really need to act wisely and rightly in our suffering. When we act improperly in our suffering, we open ourselves to unnecessary criticism. We give people things to talk about causing even more pain and heartache. Inappropriate response to pain can result in further shame and disgrace to the broken; their family, friends, church, community and even nation. Furthermore, be careful how you use Social Media when you are heartbroken. This is not the best place to vent and publicly wash your dirty linen. It can irrevocably damage your reputation and result in missed opportunities such as a promotion or employment.

18.   *Manage Your Mind*

Peter was emphatic about the need for mind management when he addressed his suffering followers. "Prepare your minds for action" (1 Pet. 3:13). Since we know that suffering is inevitable and is not a strange occurrence, it makes perfect sense to prepare our minds for action before suffering comes. Fortune favours the prepared because prior, proper planning prevents poor performance. This is exactly what Peter was telling his suffering followers. By preparing their minds ahead of time, they would be able to suffer and stand. Psychologists tell us that our thinking affects our emotions and our behaviour.

As a Christian, when you suffer, remember the great and precious promises that the King has given to us. In Peter's second letter he tells his followers to get rid of false beliefs and false teachers. Get rid of negative, fatalistic thinking. It has been said that most of our thoughts are negative. Peter exhorts us to feed ourselves with proper teaching (1 Pet. 1:4). He tells us to desire the sincere milk of God's word and to focus on good examples. He encourages us to think about the future and the goal of the faith. The entrance of God's word brings light. God sends His word and heals our diseases (Psalm 107).

Feed your mind during times of suffering and brokenness with that which is "pure, good, noteworthy, right, true and worthy of praise" (Philip. 4:8). Although it is hard to do, listen to motivational and inspirational messages. Think of past successes. Read the story of other sufferers like Nelson Mandela, Martin Luther King and others. Their stories will fortify your mind and enable you to stand.

19.   *Stay Away from Toxicity*

This also means no contact with the heartbreaker until you can regain your strength. Cut off the relationship if the situation remains unhealthy. One of Yvette's online mentors, Les Brown, teaches that we need to rid ourselves of toxic people. Toxic people will ruin your life and lead to more suffering. A counsellor once told me to cut off all contact with an abusive leader. At the time, I could not understand it but now I do. Setting limits and love go hand in hand. Why continue to play with a snake if you don't want to get bitten?

Peter warned his followers to stand guard against manipulators and those who would take advantage of them.

He warned them to stay away from false teachers who would ruin them if they listened to their teachings. In like manner, we must be careful to whom we listen when we are going through our trials and adversities. Not every advice is good or godly advice.

20. Exercise Self-Control

I am intrigued that Peter tells his suffering followers to add self-control to their faith in their time of suffering. This is difficult because we tend to lash out in pain or turn inward. Self-control is the last thing we think of when we are hurting and in pain.

When we are hurt tempers flare; we become sarcastic, make biting remarks; irritable, slanderous and selfish. We withdraw our services, gifts and abilities and isolate ourselves. We neglect our duties and pay little attention to our loved ones and the relationships around us. This leads to even greater despair. In many instances we are not conscious of our actions because the pain blinds us. But if we prepare, we can mitigate the bad effects especially with the help of our Maker and Divine Helper. This is why turning to God is most effective. Our Maker knows how to deliver the godly out of temptation (1 Peter 2:9).

> Control yourselves and be careful! The devil, your enemy, goes around like a roaring lion looking for someone to eat. Refuse to give in to him,

by standing strong in your faith. You know that your Christian family all over the world is having the same kinds of suffering (1 Peter 5:8).

We are not to succumb to evil and retaliate by seeking vigilante justice. We are naturally inclined to do in the midst of egregious suffering inflicted by others. Leave vengeance to God because the Righteous Judge of all the earth will do right. This does not mean we don't seek justice and legal intervention, but not out of malice and revenge.

21. Have Hope for the Future. Persevere and Turn it into Glory

Believe you can love again, something better is in store. Believe things will get better. Develop a vision and goals for the future. This builds resilience. This too will pass. This is not the end.

In the first chapter of Peter's first letter, he reminds his suffering followers about their living hope.

> In God's great mercy, He has caused us to be born into a living hope, because Jesus Christ rose from the dead. Now we hope for the blessings. God has for His children. These blessings, which cannot be destroyed or lose their beauty, are kept in heaven for you (1 Peter 1: 4-5).

At the close of his second letter, he gives a description of the end of the age, when the current universe will be destroyed and created anew. These are reasons to have hope: the resurrection, the return of the King, the coming judgment and rewards, and the recreation of the universe. There is hope beyond the grave.

Therefore, while we suffer now, the glory to come will outweigh the present pain. For example, many of the King's followers were killed but the King will give new life to them. When we lose loved ones, this is our blessed hope. We will be reunited. Death is not the end. Death is not the final victor. There is one who brings life from death.

The return of the King will be accompanied by rewards for the faithful. It will also result in wrath and judgment for those who continue in evil and reject the King. When the King returns, he will come as the Righteous Judge of all the earth.

Peter reminds his suffering followers that the angels who sinned did not go free without punishment. God sent them to hell and put them in caves of darkness where they are being held for judgment. He reminds his followers about the flood of Noah's time as a warning of things to come. God will punish evil people and only those who are faithful to the King, like Noah, will be saved.

He reminded them of Sodom and Gomorrah as examples of evil cities that were destroyed but Lot, the good man who lived among them was saved. He wrote the following:

The Lord knows how to save those who serve him when troubles come. He will hold evil people and punish them, while waiting for the Judgment Day. That punishment is especially for those who live by doing the evil things their sinful selves want and who hate authority (2 Peter 2: 4-10)

Peter urged his suffering followers to stand their ground. The Lord is not slow concerning his promises, and while others scoff about the delayed fulfilment of the promised return of the King, the suffering followers should not fall prey to this cynicism.

A thousand years with the King is no different from one day. The delayed return means that the King is being patient, giving people a chance to turn from their evil ways. The King wants all men to be saved. He does not want anyone to be lost (2 Peter 3: 8-9).

With the promise of life in a new universe, all pain and suffering will be a thing of the past. The Great Judge and Arbiter will pass one final sentence because vengeance belongs to him. Those who escaped punishment for earthly crimes will not escape when the King returns if they refused to change their hearts and lives while living on earth.

Those who inflict suffering and sorrow and remain unrepentant will not escape the judgment to come. Human traffickers will not escape; rapists will not escape; murderers will not escape; those who abuse their employees will not escape; those who exploit the poor will not escape; players and the sexually immoral, and those who continue in their evil ways will not escape as sure as the sun rises while earth lasts.

THE FUTURE IS BRIGHT

This is good news to sufferers especially those suffering unfairly. Their future looks bright. When we have a compelling picture of the future, it makes the pain of the present bearable. The late Jim Rohn captured this concept quite beautifully when he said, "If you know the prize, you will pay the price. If the promise of the future is clear, then you will pay the price."

If you are suffering at the hands of the wicked, your tears will not be in vain. Do not turn to suicide. Do not become bitter and hateful and self-destruct. The Judge of all the earth will do right!

I believe it was Nelson Mandela's hope in the future that caused him to endure 27 years of imprisonment. He believed one day his people would be free from the apartheid system in South Africa. He endured and achieved great success.

It was Martin Luther King's compelling vision of the future that caused him to endure much suffering in his fight for human rights for black people in the USA. In 2008, a change came: a black man, Barack Obama became president of the USA and lived in the White House. If you persevere and not give up, you will then win the prize! There is joy on the other side of pain.

Finally, turn it all into glory. "Endurance is not just the ability to bear a hard thing but to turn it into glory" – William Barclay. Yvette turned her pain into glory and so can you.

CONSOLATION AND CHALLENGE

Beloved, there are provisions, promises, patterns and practices established to enable the broken-hearted sufferer to strive and thrive instead of succumbing to defeat. Will you study and apply them to your life today?

Having knowledge and information without practice or application is useless. It produces no change or transformation. Unless you plant the fruit seed, you will never have a fruit tree although the seed is a potential tree. Only when you act upon knowledge or information does it truly become power. The choice is yours. If you are guilty of inflicting sorrow and pain, will you heed Peter's warnings? Yes, Peter was addressing a religious sect but he really believed these things are true for all people.

Beloved, in the face of inevitable suffering, I charge you like Peter did his suffering followers: "Stand strong in the grace of God." I wish you peace in every trial and may you endure and stand in the face of every suffering or heartbreak! May you be whole again!

IT IS A NEW SEASON

15.

ARE YOU WHOLE?

"So you also are complete through your union with
Christ, who is the head over every ruler and authority"
(Col. 2:10).

W hat is wholeness? What does wholeness look like? How do you know if you are whole? Up until now, we have not defined wholeness although we have been talking about a journey to wholeness. The Oxford Dictionary defines wholeness as "the state of forming a complete and harmonious whole; unity or the state of being unbroken or undamaged." While this definition is useful, it does not accurately represent the picture of wholeness envisioned in this book.

THE MARKS OF WHOLENESS

To not be whole suggests something has been broken. What is it that got broken or what is the missing part? In this sense, wholeness would be simply replacing the missing part. However, one can replace a missing part and yet not feel whole or complete. There are also instances when one feels complete even when the part is still missing. In this sense wholeness is learning to adapt or function well without the missing part. If the brokenness is a loss of a relationship, it means one does not have to replace that relationship to feel whole. If you can come to terms with the loss and move forward with a good attitude; that is evidence of wholeness.

We know replacing a missing part does not mean automatic wholeness although it could be. There are many cases where persons break up and find a new partner immediately. This rebounding relationship is often disastrous. At times, persons involved in new relationships still have issues arising from the previous loss which can hinder the progress of the new relationship. If you have dealt with the baggage of the previous loss and have a new partner, that could be evidence of wholeness. Sometimes you are so broken that you refuse to get involved again. Thus, replacing a partner in this case would be evidence of wholeness.

If you can live comfortably alone after a breakup, that is a sign of wholeness. If you get to a point of pursuing your purpose and living a meaningful life after heartbreak, that's evidence of wholeness. If the memory of the loss does not sting as much as it used to, that's a manifestation of wholeness. In fact, the pain can be completely gone even though the memories remain. It is like a scar. A scar reminds us of the hurt but when we touch it, if it heals properly, you will feel no pain. This is a great manifestation of wholeness.

If you can forgive the individuals, that's a sign of wholeness. If you are not constantly feeling regret and dwelling on the past hurt and failures, that's a manifestation of wholeness. If you can share your story without anger or bitterness, that's a manifestation of wholeness. If you are able to dream again after rejection, hurt or loss, that's a sign of wholeness. If you now have the courage to try again, that's a sign of wholeness.

The heartbreaks featured in this book include: death, loss of relationships, unmet expectations and betrayal. These are not easy to overcome. These losses cut just like a knife; the only difference is that these are internal wounds. Internal wounds often take longer to heal than physical wounds. There are 60-year old people who still struggle with issues that happened in childhood. Time does not automatically heal. Healing comes with intentional effort, support and love.

No matter what caused you to be broken, it is how you respond to the missing part that will determine your path to wholeness. It is not what happens to you; it is what you do with what happens to you. If you can thrive and create a new and fulfilling life after loss, those are signs of wholeness. Wholeness manifests itself in being willing to face your fears and confront that which caused your brokenness.

Wholeness is about making peace with your past and having a general sense of well-being. It is a state where you feel unhindered and are able to contribute and help others. When you are broken, very often you become withdrawn to block out hurt or you put up walls. **Note:** The same walls that block out hurt may also block out love. Wholeness is being willing to be vulnerable and love again.

STAGES OF WHOLENESS

Wholeness is a journey with different stages. You can be experiencing a sense of wholeness even if all pain is not gone. If the pain diminishes and does not hinder you from functioning at your best, you are on the path to wholeness. If the pain is uncontrollable, then you are still very broken. In my case, I no longer feel hurt and pain from my relational losses. I have had two broken engagements and only three positive dating relationships. For a long time, I did not see those losses as a blessing. Now I see the lessons and the blessings in them.

If the memories are less haunting, you are experiencing healing and wholeness. When it comes to heartbreak, there are different levels of brokenness. In fact, we will deal with multiple losses and new heartbreaks throughout life.

The pursuit of wholeness will be ongoing because there will be new heartbreaks and losses the longer we live. But as long as you can take charge of your life and move forward positively, then you are on your way to being whole or you are whole for the time being.

Ultimate wholeness is found in Christ Jesus. In Him we can have all that we need. He knows how to heal that which has been broken. God is the Master of wholeness. "He heals the broken-hearted and binds up their wounds" (Psalm 147: 3). I invite you to trust Him to treat your pain. I know in your brokenness, like Yvette, you may feel angry with God and blame Him for what has happened to you.

It is very hard to see any good in your situation when you are broken but if you trust God, He can make something beautiful come from it. If you are broken right now, revisit the list of 21 secrets and apply them to your life. If you have a friend who is broken and hurting, share it with them. Each time your heart breaks, read those secrets. In this way, you will have the tools to effectively deal with brokenness throughout your lifetime. Beloved, wholeness is possible! Believe it! Walk in it!

GRATEFUL ACKNOWLEDGMENTS

I give all praise and thanks to my King, Christ Jesus, who has been the God of all comfort and my gracious help, deliverer and friend. Surely without His help, I would be nothing. I would long be in the grave or gone insane. I am grateful for the Bible and its truths which guided me every step of the way.

To my immediate family, especially my mother, thanks for partnering with me on this journey! Mom, you are hands down the biggest supporter of my books. I pray that you will soon reap tangible rewards for your faith and investment over these years.

Certainly, I cannot fail to thank my unique group, my Inner Circle of wise counsellors, social support and accountability: Rev Carla Dunbar, Kevin and Shauna-Gay Gregory Edwards, Tedecia Coley, Barbara Harrison, Racquel Newman, Najwa Allen, Didan Ashanta, Davia Williams, Rev Rennard White, Rev Kenyatta Lewis, Dr Wayne Allen and Rev. Courtney Richards. You have been my rock through all my failures and victories. You have been God's special envoys to comfort, motivate and guide me at critical moments of my life.

To my endorsers, J.C. Hendee and the N.D. Author Services team [NDAS], thank you so much for teaching me about the publishing process. You have made my publishing dreams a reality by offering affordable and professional services.

Finally, to Janet Morgan and my Advanced Reading and Review Tribe (ART), thank you for proofreading the book to ensure it is error free.

ABOUT THE AUTHOR

Cameka "Ruth" Taylor is an Authorpreneurship expert, credentialled Master Teacher and Coach from the beautiful island of Jamaica. She has 20 years of experience in teaching from the Early Childhood to the Tertiary Level of the education system in Jamaica.

She's the bestselling author 20 books, including two Amazon bestsellers. She makes a full-time living from her writing and the income streams it generates.

As an Independent Publisher, Ruth not only publishes her own books but has helped many Caribbean authors to make their publishing dreams a reality, by breaking down the price barrier to entry and simplifying the publishing process.

She is on a mission to ensure fewer books die in the minds of their authors, that more manuscripts become published legacies and precious lives are transformed with the turn of each page.

She is committed to helping more people in the Caribbean and the African Diaspora to write, publish and share our stories and expertise as well as declare God's glory among the nations.

Through the Authorpreneurship Academy and the books and resources she develops, Ruth teaches authors and leaders how to create greater impact, income and influence with non-fiction books.

With over 17 years of speaking and travelling experience across 14 countries, Ruth continues to activate, educate and empower thousands of people in Jamaica, other countries in the Caribbean region, Latin America and Africa to win in their personal, professional and spiritual lives for the glory of God.

Contact her at ruthtaylor@extramileja.com if you need her coaching, writing, publishing or speaking services. You may also visit her website www.extramileja.com to read her blogs and learn more about her endeavours.

NOTE: If you found this material helpful, please submit a review on the platform where you purchased it. You can also send feedback to the author. Thank you.

NOTES

CHAPTER 6

1. Seamands, David A. *Healing for Damaged Emotions: Recovering from the Memories that Cause our Pain.* USA, 1991.

2. Clarke, David. *The 6 Steps to Emotional Freedom: Breaking Through to the Life God Wants You to Live.* Uhrichsville, Ohio: 2007. Renamed and Reprinted as *I'm Not Ok and Neither are You: 6 Steps to Emotional Freedom*

CHAPTER 7

1.   African Craft Markets. *Ashanti People, Tradition and Cultures.* Web. May 8, 2014. http://www.africancraftsmarket.com/Ashanti_people. htm

CHAPTER 8

1. Earle Nightingale. *Lead the Field Series.* Web. https://www.youtube.com/ watch?v=HUUrnCmFzFs

CHAPTER 9

1. Values.Com. Web. May 5, 2014. http://www.values.com/inspirational-quotes/4742-Our-Deepest-Fear-Is-Not-Tha Vuijic, Nick. Attitude is Altitude/Life Without Limbs. Web. https://www.youtube.com/watch?v=AJvEoLPLIg8

2. Anderson, Neil T. Steps to Freedom in Christ. USA: Bethany House Publisher, 2001.

CHAPTER 10

1. Callahan, Allan D. The Political Climate of Galilee. 1998. Web. http://www.pbs.org/wgbh/pages/frontline/shows/religion/portrait/galilee. html.

2. The Bible. St John 21.

3. The New Analytical Bible and Dictionary Bible: Authorized King
James Version, Outstanding Facts. Grand Rapids, Michigan: World Publishing, 1973.

CHAPTER 11
1. Thesaurus.com. Suffering. Web. May 7, 2014. http://dictionary. reference.com/browse/suffering

2. Hill, Napoleon. Think and Grow Rich. Web. May 7, 2014. https://www.youtube.com/watch?v=QoUVhKpLwXQ.

3. Rohn, Jim. The Set of the Sail. Web. May 7, 2014. https://www.youtube. com/watch?v=5k4Il-xG98Y

RESOURCES BY C. RUTH TAYLOR

Visit www.extramileja.com/home to get a free e-copy of my bestselling book "Design to Win Road Map" to chart your journey to win at life.

If you are interested in Authorpreneurship, join our free Facebook tribe "Indie Authorpreneurs" to learn how to publish on a budget, create multiple income streams and impact more lives with books. Upon joining, you will get a 1-page pre-publishing checklist and other goodies. Subscribe to Ruth's YouTube Channel to learn some Authorpreneur secrets and powerful, proven keys to win in your life and career.

Ruth's Fearless 40 Series

This is a collection of eBooks including *Unshackled Queen* to celebrate Ruth's 40th birthday in May 2020. They are designed to help persons who are approaching age 40 and those over 40 years of age, to slay their fears, revive their courage to dream again and soar to new heights in their later years. The other books in the series are listed on page below.

1. *Design to Win Road Map 2: How to Dream Again and Succeed in Life as You Get Older [Late Bloomers' Edition]*

2. *Embracing Destiny: 21 Pep Talks to Walk in Your Greatness*

3. *Embracing Singleness: Secrets to Maximize and Enjoy It While It Lasts.*

4. *Fearless 40: Secrets to Slay Fear and Soar to New Heights as You Get Older*

5. *Pen It to Win It: Going Beyond Book Sales*

You can find several of Ruth's other books on Amazon and other digital publishing platforms. Visit www.extramileja.com/ruths-bookshop/ to get your copy of the *Fearless 40 Ebook Series* and tell your friends about the series.

www.ingramcontent.com/pod-product-compliance
Lightning Source LLC
Chambersburg PA
CBHW032002040426
42448CB00006B/457